SAGA OF THE
RED TRUCK

Life Lessons From Here and There

SAGA OF THE
RED TRUCK

Life Lessons From Here and There

G. ROGER SCHOENHALS

REDEMPTION
PRESS

Published by Redemption Press, PO Box 427, Enumclaw, WA 98022
Toll Free (844) 2REDEEM (273-3336)

Redemption Press is honored to present this title in partnership with the author. The views expressed or implied in this work are those of the author. Redemption Press provides our imprint seal representing design excellence, creative content and high quality production.

ISBN 13: 978-1-63232-995-0

Library of Congress Catalog Card Number: 2016931169

Dedication

To granddaughter Naomi
who will someday write
of her own adventures.

Contents ℮～

Introduction ix

Chapter 1: Moms Know 11
Chapter 2: Water Balloons and TP 17
Chapter 3: On the Canal 23
Chapter 4: Unintended Consequences 29
Chapter 5: The Paperboy 33
Chapter 6: Troop 68 39
Chapter 7: The Pain of Betrayal 45
Chapter 8: Waxing Eloquent for Fun 49
Chapter 9: Great Falls 55
Chapter 10: Episodes of Help 61
Chapter 11: Living With Pests 67
Chapter 12: When Prince Went Berserk 73
Chapter 13: First Aid in the Wilderness 81
Chapter 14: The Dingford Creek Fire 85
Chapter 15: Surprised By Fire 93
Chapter 16: Rattlers Near Home 97

Chapter 17: An "Alarming" Story 101
Chapter 18: Saga of the Red Truck. 105
Chapter 19: Auto Mishaps 109
Chapter 20: Skunk in the Parsonage. 115
Chapter 21: The Yucky Tongue 121
Chapter 22: Spring Break. 125
Chapter 23: Living in Joy Hall. 133
Chapter 24: Odd Jobs 137
Chapter 25: Cool Thoughts. 143
Chapter 26: Breaking Stride. 147
Chapter 27: Losing Cause 151
Chapter 28: When Mom Stomped Out 157
Chapter 29: Goodbye, Old Friend 161
Chapter 30: Two Batons. 167

About the Author. 171

Introduction

Saga of the Red Truck—*Life Lessons From Here and There* is the third book of stories from my life. This book, more than the others, is a hodgepodge of happenings. Many of them come from my earlier years. Though I have tried to connect the chapters in a way that provides some small measure of flow from subject to subject, you may justly conclude that my efforts in this regard failed miserably.

I am always amazed with memories stored away in our minds. When I completed my first book of 30 stories, I thought I had exhausted all the material. Then I started the second book and the more I delved into my past, the more I discovered episodes to recount. Now here is yet another book. Perhaps this is a case of the aging process when short-term memory wanes and long-term memory comes alive.

Some of my favorite stories are in this book—things that had slipped my mind completely. For example, there was the Sunday morning when I tossed water balloons on parishioners from the church bell tower. And the time I visited an abandoned outhouse and sat on a hornet's nest. And the afternoon I ventured out onto the Lake Washington Ship Canal on a homemade raft.

As in the earlier books, you'll find that I end each story with a moral or spiritual connection. I hope you find this helpful in applying the experiences to your own life. After all, life itself is a schoolroom that teaches us about values and how to live in a worthwhile way.

In these pages you will discover honest reporting of my errors of judgment and some just plain dumb decisions. At times you may wince or laugh, or perhaps even experience some inspiration. All of the stories are true.

Life is a long walk along a narrow road and we need all the help we can get to make our final Destination safely. Someday, through our faith in Christ, we will hobnob with angels and glory in the nearer presence of our Lord. I guess you might say that getting to Heaven in one piece is what this book is all about.

If you enjoy these stories, you will probably like my earlier collections of stories titled, *Hikes, Flights, and Lookout Stories—Life Lessons From High Places,* and *Dogs, Camping, and Other Candid Tales—Life Lessons From the Out-of-Doors.* You will find information about these and my other books at www. papathree.com.

You may wonder about the cover photo and where the story of the red truck appears in the book. You'll find it in chapter 18. For now, let's start out with "Mom's Know," a story of my youthful efforts to extract contributions from neighbors under the guise of raising money for missionaries.

Chapter 1

Moms Know ℰ∽

For some reason it is easier for me to recall negative episodes of my youth than those things that yielded positive reward. Maybe the good was so rare that it has been lost in obscurity, whereas the other things occurred in such abundance that they spill out of my memory easily. In any case, I feel compelled to relate stories of the past, if for no other reason than to redeem them through spiritual application to contemporary life.

Today I am recalling my shameful behavior as a childhood fundraiser. I must have been six or seven at the time the following sham occurred.

It started in Sunday school. We were given little piggybanks and urged to go home and put in some of our pennies and nickels for a month and then bring back the banks for a missionary project.

Being something of a scoundrel, my young mind saw unlimited possibilities in this pennies-for-missions program. If I could get other people to put money in my bank, I could use some of it to buy candy. You might call it fundraising overhead. Visions of goodies danced in my mind.

Monday, after school, I set out to cover the neighborhood. I marched up to the first porch, rang the bell, and waited for the prospect to appear. Then I held out the bank and said something like, "I'm raising money for a Sunday school project. It's for missionaries in Africa. Do you want to put something in the bank to help?" Bingo! She put in several coins.

I went to the second house and scored again. Soon I had five houses and five donations. What a deal!

I couldn't wait to spend part of the loot, so I headed off to the corner grocery store. I'd canvass the rest of the neighborhood tomorrow.

On the way home, I stuffed my pockets with the candy and threw away the sack. I didn't want anyone to know where I'd been. If I could just get to my bedroom and stash the candy without detection, I'd be home free—as it were.

Of course I left a few pennies in the bank for the mission's project. After all, I didn't want to stand out as a failure when the teacher collected the banks.

Meanwhile, one of the donors got suspicious and called my mother. This woman was struggling with dissonance as she tried to reconcile my meek little missionary appeal with my dubious reputation as the "terror" of the neighborhood. Was there really a mission's project?

I walked in the door and ran into Mom. Next came the "look-into-my-eyes" interrogation conducted in our kitchen. I never could handle my mom's penetrating gaze, so I crumbled and confessed.

Part of my punishment included a door-to-door confession. Another part involved chores to earn the money I had spent so I could replenish the piggybank for missions. As I recall, another aspect of my punishment had something to do with the seat of my pants.

That early encounter with fundraising fraud cured me good...and I like to believe I've been clean ever since. Yet, sometimes I wonder whether I'm as pure as I should be in other areas of my adult life.

For example, do I accept unwarranted reward? Do I take all the credit for something I didn't do singlehandedly? It may seem a small thing, but on the purity scale it qualifies as dishonesty. Collecting the praise of man under false pretense is unbecoming a follower of Christ.

My fraudulent piggybank fundraising scheme was despicable because I deceived others for personal gain. My mother was absolutely right in her (and my dad's) response. Sometimes, as adults, we would do well to have trusted friends or family help us "walk the line" in both our public and private lives.

On another occasion it was a friend's mother who called me to task. I was visiting a friend who lived on a farm a few hours from Seattle. During the night, when the house was quiet and we were supposedly asleep, we crept outside armed with a few newspapers and a box of matches.

We walked up the two-lane country road a ways and watched in the distance for the approach of a car. Then we wadded some papers, placed them in the center of the road, lit the fuel, and hid in the bushes to see what would happen. One driver might slow and steer around the flame, while another might stop to see what was burning. One guy got out and stamped out the fire.

When the "fun" of that activity waned, we walked into the yard of a house belonging to two elderly sisters. We tossed the papers on the lawn and gathered some rocks. These we threw onto the steep metal roof, causing a racket as the rocks rolled down. The sound drew attention and lights came on. We ran back home and climbed into bed like two innocent cherubs.

The next morning, my friend's mom addressed us in the kitchen. "Did you boys go out last night after you went to bed?"

Shocked to the core, we nonetheless pretended innocence and asked why she would think such a thing.

Then this rather large and stern German woman related the phone call she had received earlier in the morning. It seems the two sisters went outside to investigate and found some papers on the lawn. These papers, earlier delivered by mail, bore the name and address of my friend's mom and dad.

Busted! Appropriately disciplined, we were also required to go to the sisters and apologize for our egregious behavior.

The moral, I am sure, underscores the ancient maxim: "Be sure your sins will find you out."

Even though we may think we have eluded detection in some act of misconduct, the truth is that God knows and that we stand condemned in his presence—even for the smallest infraction or wrongdoing. We are born as sinful creatures and we live sinful lives either through commission of evil deeds or the omission of righteous behavior.

However—and this is the grandest news of all time—God who is rich in mercy, even when we fall short of his glory, loves us immeasurably and calls us to the cross where our sins are washed away. Our heavenly Father earnestly desires to apply his forgiveness to our hearts if we will only confess our sins and trust in his marvelous grace.

We may have graduated from prankish behavior, only to become more sophisticated in our wrongdoings and deceptions. The fact is, we never outgrow our need for mercy and grace.

So let us celebrate the ongoing, unlimited, and deep, deep love of Jesus. Let us walk before him in the beauty of his holiness and live in the knowledge that our sins have been buried in the deepest sea, never to be remembered against us again.

Chapter 2

Water Balloons and TP

I grew up attending a church across the street from Seattle Pacific College (now a university). In the 40s, the church building was a large wooden edifice with a commanding bell-tower. On Sunday mornings, the custodian pulled on the long rope to ring the bell. The whole neighborhood knew it was time to come to church.

As soon as I was young enough to figure things out, I located the "secret" door that led to the ladder one could climb up into the belfry. I remember going up there and, amid all the pigeon droppings, looking down to the sidewalk and out over the campus.

It was during one such visit to the belfry that a friend and I concocted the idea of using this lofty place as a launching pad for water balloons. The next Sunday we met in the lavatory and filled several balloons with water. Then, before church was out, we climbed to the belfry and baptized unsuspecting parishioners as they exited the building.

I had pushed this incident out of my mind until a few years ago when one of the balloon recipients reminded me of that fateful day. I said it was probably _____ who did it. "No," she said, "it was you. I remember it quite well."

Within the space of a year, another elderly person spoke of the incident. Fortunately, she laughed as she recounted the stir I caused. I doubt she thought it was funny at the time.

I don't recall my punishment for that Sunday morning transgression, but I can guarantee you my dad fulfilled his parental responsibilities.

It was during the same creative time in my youth when I decided to construct a club house in the basement of our house. While my folks were away, I gathered all the bits and pieces of wood I could find and began nailing them onto the wall of our basement. I picked a corner, thinking I could at least have two sides looking rustic. Then I'd hang blankets from the ceiling for the other two sides.

By the time my folks returned, I was nearly done with one wall and feeling pretty proud of my handiwork. Unfortunately, my enthusiasm and craftsmanship failed to impress my dad. Again, I can report that my punishment was likely commensurate with my crime.

I was a slow learner, because it wasn't long after that construction project that I decided to dig a swimming pool in the back yard. With the help of a few pals, we shoveled out a hole that was probably six-feet square and a couple feet deep. Then we turned on the hose and let the water run and run and run. Eventually we had enough water to splash in wearing our bathing suits.

Of course, the "pool" turned into a mud hole and we bathers turned a dark brown. It was a mess, and tracking mud into the house only exacerbated the situation.

When Dad came home he dismissed the neighbor kids and set me to shoveling the dirt back into the hole. Not once did he thank me for performing a property upgrade that would surely raise the value of our property. Nor did he express gratitude for my thoughtfulness in providing a recreational resource for the neighborhood.

My father served as the primary disciplinarian in our home. Mom would say something like, "Wait till your father comes home and hears about this." The waiting part was almost as bad as the punishment part.

I do not recall my father spanking me in anger; but I do remember his firm application of posterior justice. He would explain why he was punishing me and then he would administer a few swats on the backside. Afterward I would be sent upstairs to my room, sometimes without dinner.

I'd lay there in bed feeling sorry for myself until later in the evening when I'd hear my dad's footsteps on the stairs. He'd come into my room and sit on my bed and say something like, "Spanking you hurts me more than it hurts you." Yeah, right.

He would tell me that he loved me and that he wanted me to grow up into a fine young man. He'd pat me and say goodnight and turn off the light as he closed the door. I'd listen to him descending the stairs...and then I would drift off to sleep wanting to be a good boy.

My dad directed the concert choir at Seattle Pacific College and each year the choir would go on tour during spring vacation. My mother went as well, and that meant that my sister and I were placed in the hands of babysitters.

One year during choir tour we were cared for by a young married couple who attended SPC. With my parents out of town and our sitters in classes, I decided to take a day off from school. I think I was in the first grade.

Burt—a neighbor friend down the block—agreed to join me. We left home as usual with our lunch boxes and pretended to walk the two blocks to school as we always did. Along the way, however, we darted into some bushes and craftily snuck to an empty lot where there was lots of cover.

There we sat on the ground eating the good stuff from the lunch boxes, as well as some candy Burt had brought along. We talked and laughed and had a good time. At least until we heard rustling in the bushes.

"Roger, are you in there?" It was the voice of the husband babysitter.

"Roger, I know your there! Come on out!"

Sheepishly, we came into the light. There we received a brief lecture about scaring everyone by our absence and what it required of the principal to find my guardian at SPC. He was controlled, but definitely not happy about our truancy.

He marched both of us to the school and to the principal's office where we were further lectured on the evils of hooky. Burt's mom had been called and was on her way.

The incident was also reported to my parents and though they were out of state at the time a plethora of serious words reached my ears through the telephone. It was years before I even thought of skipping school again.

As I grew older, I developed a bit more finesse in my mischief-making. For example, during my early teen years I sometimes rode my bike to visit a friend who lived in an exclusive neighborhood five or six miles away. Perched on a bluff overlooking Puget Sound, this exquisite home was kept immaculate, always ready to entertain important guests who would come to see my friend's parents.

One time, while using the guest bathroom, I had a sudden inspiration. I unrolled 20 or 30 feet of toilet paper and then printed, in pen, "Hi!" on a leaf of paper. On another I printed, "Smile, You're On Candid Camera." And on another, "Kilroy Was Here." Then, with utmost care, I rewound the TP to its original condition.

I never heard what happened...but my imagination has taken me on flights that even now evoke a smile.

I don't know about your childhood and whether you regret some of your activities. You may have lived a very quiet life, free of disturbance or prankish antics. Or maybe your past runs circles around my occasional indiscretions. Whatever the case, apart from obvious exceptions, our individuality is something to be celebrated and affirmed. We are wonderfully unique.

God our Father is longsuffering and masterful. He disciplines us in love and encourages us through his Word and the words of others. He says to our hearts, "Son or daughter, the cross hurt me more than you will ever know. I love you and I am at work in you to use all your experiences—good and ill—to mold you into a one-of-a-kind vessel, pure and holy, fit for my personal use."

We are children of the Most High God and what he has begun in us he will continue to perfect until the Day we rise to meet him in the air.

Chapter 3

On the Canal ℰ

I grew up on the lower north side of Queen Anne Hill in Seattle.
A few blocks away, the Lake Washington Ship Canal carried
boat traffic from Lake Washington to Puget Sound. Since the
elevation of the lake sits above the Sound, government locks
were installed in 1917 to raise and lower the water level so boats
could get from the salt water to the fresh water, and visa-versa. A
slow but steady current moves from the lake toward the Sound.

Ships that have been at sea collect barnacles and some of
these vessels are brought through the canal to fresh water where
the barnacles die and fall off the hull. It's quite impressive to see
one of these ships move through the narrow canal.

There are many fresh water marinas where all sorts of boats
are moored. Most of these are pleasure crafts used only on the
weekends. On holiday weekends a boat may have to wait one
or two hours to get through the locks.

There are two sections of the canal separated by a small
lake near downtown Seattle. Four drawbridges cross the canal.
Two—Montlake and University—span the canal nearest Lake

Washington. Both of these bridges are near the University of Washington. The other two bridges—Fremont and Ballard—are closer to the locks. Seattle Pacific University is located half way between these bridges.

When a sailboat with a tall mast or one of the larger boats approaches a bridge, the captain toots a horn. Some of these toots sound pretty feeble. The bridge operator acknowledges with a long and short blast and the gates come down to stop car traffic. Then the two halves of the bridge rise and the boat passes through. The whole process is actually quite fast and goes smoothly. Fremont is the lower of the four bridges, which means it actually goes up and down more than the other three. It is, in fact, the busiest bridge in the U.S., opening an average of 35 times a day.

As you might expect, the canal at the foot of Queen Anne Hill became a playground for several of us during our younger years. We would occasionally swim in the yucky water or stand on the bank and watch the boats go by.

In one section of the canal, a series of houseboats floated near the shore. Whereas today this would be seen as prime property, in the 1940s and 50s it was inhabited by the less fortunate of society. The shacks floated on logs and bobbed with the waves created by passing boats.

When my sister was three-and-a-half years old, she wandered away from home and walked two blocks to the campus where my dad worked. Along the way she met a young friend who said, "Let's go down to the canal."

When they got there, they climbed up onto the bulkhead and started to walk single file along the canal. That's when she fell into the water and her friend ran away. A man on the opposite side of the canal, who was fishing, saw it happen and began yelling across the water for help. Another man working nearby heard the yell and went to investigate. He jumped in and rescued Stephanie, who was standing on a sandy bar with her head just above the water. The incident made the newspapers and my parents gave thanks to God.

Perhaps as a result of my sister's close call, my folks made doubly sure I was well in tow during my early years. However, when I hit the upper levels of grade school I learned how to elude my parents and sneak down to the canal to explore and experiment.

Farther down the canal, closer to the government locks, a sawmill operated near the Ballard Bridge. Logs would be brought either through the locks or from Lake Washington in "booms" for processing. There might be three or four booms of 100 logs each tied to pilings near the mill. It was fun to watch the employees hop around the logs, moving them this way and that. At times a worker would have to "logroll" to keep from falling in the water.

The fun of watching soon changed to the fun of doing it ourselves. On weekends, when the mill was quiet, a few of us would sneak into the area with the log booms and try our hand at logrolling. We adroitly ran across the logs and had various competitions. For example, two of us would get on a log and roll it until one fell off into the water. Sometimes I'd go down to the mill on a Sunday afternoon by myself and roll logs. As I look back on those carefree times, I'm amazed that the Lord saw fit to preserve my life into adulthood.

I mentioned the houseboat neighborhood where a dozen or so shacks floated near the shore. I got acquainted with a few of these folks and did some carp fishing from the walkways leading to the shacks. One day I saw a few loose logs floating in the area and thought, *I will build myself a raft.*

I went home and gathered a few items for the raft: rope to hold the logs together and a piece of plywood to serve as a small platform. At the site, I found a wooden box to sit on and a long piece of wood to use as a paddle.

Wearing a swimsuit and tennis shoes, I used a long pole to work the logs close to the dock. Then I did my best to attach them together and put my platform and "captain's chair" in place. With a few of the residents looking on, I gingerly moved from the dock to the raft. I untied the moorage rope and floated free. What a feeling! As I paddled out toward the canal I felt like Tom Sawyer going on the adventure of a lifetime.

It was then I discovered two salient facts: The current was stronger than my ability to propel the raft; and the wake of passing boats disturbed the water significantly. The roll of the waves under my raft moved the logs around, causing them to break free. I tumbled into the water and swam for shore downstream from where I started.

Again, I marvel at the mercy of the Lord.

I think of the little rafts we construct throughout our lives—ill-conceived plans to navigate our way along the canal from confined lake to eternal sea. Homemade vessels of faulty belief and false assertions. We think we are the master of our ship when in reality we are like a chip of wood tossed this way and that by waves and wind.

Like the disciples on Lake Galilee, we despair when the storm comes. Like Peter, we slip into the deep when we turn our gaze from Jesus to the whitecaps at our feet.

On the Canal

Again and again we are reminded of our continuing need to sail the ship of faith and to trust Christ to deliver us from temptations, wrong choices, negative attitudes, and pride. Living in him we discard the barnacles of disbelief and selfish attachments. In him we ride the current of life safe and secure. He is our seaworthy vessel and our shelter in the time of storm.

Jesus, Savior, pilot me
Over life's tempestuous sea.

Chapter 4

Unintended Consequences

Some of my unforgettable experiences occurred during family vacations or one day get-a-ways when we piled in the car and headed out of town. A few of these family times are particularly noteworthy due to the unintended consequences of my behavior.

For example, one winter Saturday Dad decided to take us up to Stevens Pass to play in the snow. I was probably six or seven at the time. My special super-duper Red Flyer sled was packed in the trunk, along with winter coats and a bountiful lunch. Another family joined us in their car and together we headed out of Seattle for snow country.

My excitement grew with every mile and by the time we arrived, I was bouncing around inside the car. As soon as Dad parked the car I bounded out of the door, ran around to the trunk, and threw opened the lid to retrieve the sled. As I reached in, the trunk lid came crashing down on my head, causing an immediate flow of blood.

After a brief panic attack, my dad put a cloth on my head and Mom held it there while he and the others unpacked the car. "I'm going to take him down to the emergency room in Monroe," Dad said. "You go ahead and have a good time and we'll be back in a few hours."

After a few stitches we returned to Stevens Pass where I watched the others play in the snow with my sled.

Another time when I managed to spoil a vacation took place during a camping trip at the Dosewallips River Campground in the Olympic National Park. We set up two pup tents at the campsite—one for Mom and Dad and the other for my sister and me. Again, I was probably around six or seven.

After we roasted the obligatory marshmallows, everyone went to bed. I stayed behind to watch the dying flames and to wait until my sister was snuggled in her sleeping bag. Then, I stealthily made my way around the back of our tent where I planned to kneel down and make menacing noises and growl like a bear in Stephanie's ear. This would scare the bejeebers out of her.

However, before reaching my destination, I tripped over a tent peg and went sprawling forward, driving another peg into my underarm. My screams filled the campground and Dad flew out of his tent like a startled Cheetah. He packed me in the car and rushed me to the nearest health facility. The wound looked worse than it was and we were back at the campsite before long. I've sublimated the lecture I must have received during the ride back.

Another experience comes to mind during a vacation on Orcas Island in the San Juan archipelago. We were staying with some friends in their rustic cabin and I was fascinated with the little building out back. It was called an "outhouse" and had not been used after the cabin acquired indoor plumbing several years before.

A five-year-old can be mighty curious, so it wasn't long before I decided to use the outhouse for my own needs. Opening the door and dropping my drawers, I crawled onto the seat and discovered almost immediately a hornet's nest beneath me. I came out of that outhouse falling over my pants and yowling like a scalded cat.

Everyone piled out of the cabin at once to fetch me from the attacking hornets and get me safely to the house. I do not recall the sting count, but I am sure my pincushion bottom was sore for days.

Then there was the time we were camping in Yellowstone National Park. I'm guessing I was around seven or eight. Late one afternoon I was wandering around the campground when a man came by with a string of fish. He said something like, "Sonny, how would you like to have these fish? I have more than I can eat and I bet your mom can fix these up for dinner. Do you think you can use them?"

"Oh yes," I said. "Thank you very much. These will taste great!"

When I strutted into our campsite and showed the fish to my folks, they asked where they came from. I told them about the nice man and how he said these would make a fine meal.

Mom had already begun dinner and neither she nor my dad had any interest in cleaning and fixing the fish. To my disappointment, the fish were placed in a garbage can and we ate our hotdogs and beans.

The next morning we were sitting around the campfire when the man who had given me the fish came by. "How did those trout taste? Did you enjoy them?"

While Mom and Dad looked bewildered, as if searching for the right words, I blurted out, "We threw them away!"

When the man left, a brief lecture ensued. I think it was something about children being seen and not heard.

There are morals to each of these stories, as I am sure you can divine. The first one might be a lesson in patience. Sometimes it's better to take things slowly and let others help. I was denied a full day of fun in the snow simply because I rushed ahead of the others. Further, my rash behavior caused worry and inconvenience for others.

The dastardly scheme to scare my sister resulted in another ordeal for others. I thought I was being clever, but my actions led to alarm and distress. Ill-considered practical jokes have a way of backfiring.

Doubtless, the unfortunate trip to the outhouse has a moral, but I'm not going to look for it. You're on your own.

Finally, sometimes it is better to refuse a gift than to take it and toss it away. I think of the many blessings of God that we eagerly receive, only to let them waste away through misuse or neglect. When we receive good gifts from our Heavenly Father, it may require a change in menu so we can feast on the better food of Heaven. A few "fish," blessed by God, can amply feed us and a multitude beside.

Chapter 5

The Paperboy

For several years in my youth, I carried newspapers door to door. During one stretch of time, I had four paper routes: The Seattle Times, The Seattle Post Intelligencer, The Shopping News, and The Queen Anne News. Three of these routes required me to go to the front door every month and collect money. All of the routes were on the north side of Queen Anne Hill.

The Seattle PI was a morning paper and this required getting up at the crack of dawn to deliver papers before school. The Seattle Times had a morning delivery on Sunday, and so on that day I did two routes before breakfast.

Do you know what happens when a paperboy gets sick? Mom and Dad come to the rescue—not willingly, mind you, but dependably as the need arose. I remember my Mom driving the car around while I stumbled out the door to toss the paper toward the porch. And there were times when my dad, the college professor, actually delivered the papers in my stead.

We talk about mail carriers slogging through rain, sleet, and snow, but they don't have anything over those young kids who home-deliver papers every day (including weekends).

Once I burned my finger at home and could only find relief by keeping the wounded digit in water. So, when I delivered the papers that day, I carried a plastic cup full of water with my finger dangling in the water the entire route.

Every month it was time to collect. I'd go up to the porch, ring the bell, and stand there expectantly. If the residents were gone, I'd have to return again and maybe even a third or fourth time. Sometimes I think they knew it was me and just didn't come to the door.

I had some customers who took all three papers requiring collection. I liked to go to those houses because I'd walk away a rich man. Of course, I had to share some of my income with the paper publishers, but I still came out pretty well for a young teen.

What I recall most from those years as a paperboy are the encounters I had, not with people on the porch, but with dogs in the yard. I can say from firsthand experience I know what it means to elude a jaw-snapping pursuer.

One time—and I recall this vividly—I entered a yard where I met an unfriendly bulldog. He came straight at me and I held out the front of my paper bag to protect myself. The dog clamped its teeth onto the bag and started to pull. I held the other end and a tug-of-war ensued, papers flying everywhere. Finally, perhaps in response to my yelling, someone came out of the house and delivered me from the bulldog. I gathered my papers, stuffed them into my torn bag, and bid the dog and onlookers adieu.

I got bit once on the calf of my leg. The next day I armed myself with a pocket of rocks to ward off the mean mutt. I met the dog again and this time struck back. The dog never bothered me again.

Over time, I came to realize that some dog owners use a rolled-up newspaper to punish their dogs. Then I'd come along with a rolled-up paper to fling on the porch and the dogs would go berserk.

During those years I befriended a neighbor's dog named Danny. Actually, I think he befriended me. He was a cross between a Collie and German Shepherd and he seemed to enjoy accompanying me on my routes. He was protective and so my problems with hostile dogs diminished significantly when Danny was along.

I mentioned earlier how my parents were occasionally drawn into my paper route business during sickness. There were other occasions as well. For example, one time I was delivering papers to an area near our home when I came upon some friends playing baseball in the yard. I laid my paper bag aside and joined them for a while. My time to bat arrived and I connected mightily, so much so that the ball went out of the yard and through the window of a senior-housing apartment building next door.

An elderly woman came out with vengeance in her eyes and my friends pointed to me in unison. The bottom line is that my dad, the professor, personally replaced the window. I don't recall my punishment, but I am sure it was commensurate with my deed.

Sometimes I would have extra Seattle Times papers at the end of my afternoon route. I'd go down to a busy intersection near the Fremont Bridge. When I say busy, I'm talking about five or six roads converging in a maze of traffic lights, signs, and separation islands. Horns honked and cars maneuvered this way and that.

Rush hour was a veritable circus. I'd get out there among the traffic, hold up a paper and yell, "Paper! Paper! Read all about it!" I'd yell out the headlines and watch for the least bit of interest from a driver. It was easy to get rid of extra papers that way and I was able to pocket the entire amount.

One might think that four paper routes are more than enough. However, there were times when I also substituted for another carrier who was on vacation. I guess you'd say I was a paperboy junkie.

Periodically, the publishers would sponsor contests to get new subscriptions. On those occasions I'd switch from delivery to marketing. I'd go up to the porch and try to connect with the occupant who came to the door and didn't want to talk to a pushy kid. After a while I learned some tricks that engaged the adults and won them over. One year I sold so many subscriptions for the Seattle PI that I won a nice prize and got my photo in the paper.

Occasionally, when I'm in Seattle, I drive around the old neighborhood and recall some of my experiences as a paperboy. It seems so long ago. Well, actually, it is. I also drive through that horrid traffic area near the Fremont Bridge and think how lucky I was to get through those afternoons alive.

As I think about my paper route days I am reminded of the Good News of the Gospel and our high calling to deliver the news of God's love to others. I think of the purpose this gives to life and the challenges along the way—the stairs of resistance, the barking dogs of opposition, and the rain, snow and sleet of discomfort.

And I think of the Holy Spirit who is always with us to cheer us on the way, and to protect us from the unseen enemies of darkness. I think of honest work and the good feeling of doing something worthwhile.

It's dangerous to mingle among the traffic of life, trying to interest people in the Good News. The world rushes by, intent on empty destinations. We stand among the noise and danger, calling out through word and deed, "Bible! Bible! Read all about it! God is love! God is love!"

Troop 68

Like many young men, I went through Cub Scouts and Boy Scouts. Each phase brought new experiences and adventures. I never made it to Eagle Scout—in fact, I don't recall any of my contemporaries reaching that lofty goal. I did acquire several merit badges, though, and wore the patches proudly on my uniform.

Boy Scout Troop 68 met in the basement of the church educational unit and used the back alley for fire-building and other outdoor training activities. I particularly liked the nights we competed against each other to see who could win the string-burning contest.

The scoutmaster would break us into teams of two. Each team would then place two posts in the ground about two-feet apart. Then we'd stretch a string between the two wood sticks 18 inches above ground. A pile of wood was nearby to be used as fuel. Each team received two matches, as well as a hatchet and a pocket knife. No other materials were permitted.

Our goal was to build a fire between the two posts that would flame high enough to burn through the string. Each team would talk over strategy and assign tasks. We'd consider time, efficiency, and teamwork. It was all very serious stuff for us.

When the fire sites were inspected and measurements checked, the scoutmaster would blow a whistle and we'd fly into action. Woe to the team that didn't take enough time to gather a sufficient amount of wood shavings. Woe to those who spent too much time laying the fire before striking a match. And woe to the hapless scouts who used up both matches without starting a fire.

The first team to burn through the string was declared winner. The others would vow to take the title next time. That year, at a regional Boy Scout campout, our troop won first prize in the string-burning competition.

We had terrific leaders and we all wanted to emulate them. I remember one guy, a college student, who had muscles on top of his muscles. He had no trouble keeping us in line.

One night a new adult showed up to assist the other leaders. None of us knew him, but one of the leaders did and invited him to come and help out. At least that's the way I recall it.

We liked this new guy. One night he was showing us some jujitsu moves when his wallet fell out of his pocket. One of us looked in it and saw several hundred dollar bills. Someone said, "What do you do, rob banks." He said, "Yes," and we all chuckled.

I think that was the night he took us out to see his car—a suped-up sedan that sat restlessly at the curb. He raised the hood and we all gawked.

A week or so later we learned that this "leader" had been arrested for driving the getaway car in a bank robbery. Meanwhile, the scoutmaster had some explaining to do to our parents.

That brief association with the new guy taught us something important: Choose your heroes carefully.

One night some of us were in an unfinished room in the basement that was surrounded by cement block walls. No scout leader was present, so one of the guys took a .22 shell out of his pocket. He thought it would be neat to throw it against the wall to see what would happen. I think it was the third try when the shell fired and the slug ricocheted around the room. Not a particularly smart thing to do. Fortunately, no one was hurt. None of us ever did anything like that again.

I remember my first camping experience as a neophyte scout. We went to an abandoned military facility on Whidbey Island called "Fort Casey." It had been constructed along with two other forts across Puget Sound to provide a triangular defense against enemy ships that might sail into U.S. waters through the Straights of Juan de Fuca during World War I. Huge gun emplacements and underground tunnels made it a fascinating place for a group of young teens.

However, what stands out most in my memory was the breakfast I tried to fix the next morning. I was going to make eggs and bacon over a little fire, using my new mess kit. A problem occurred when I tried to cook before getting the fire going well. The pan never did heat up enough to fry the contents and my culinary efforts turned out to be a gross-looking combination of runny eggs and raw bacon. My comrades thought it was hilarious.

I recall a hiking trip a few years later when we climbed into a highland lake in the rain. We expected the weather to change for the good but, of course, that didn't happen. What was worse was our failure to get a fire started. Everything was soaking wet and try as we might, the string-burning training we had received failed to work in the rain.

One year one of the dads encouraged us to sell Christmas trees. He thought it would provide good experience in business matters. We had a corner lot to use and so we pooled our meager resources, borrowed from our folks, and purchased a bunch of trees wholesale. We put up signs and assigned shifts to guard the trees and collect the funds we were sure would come rolling in from supportive neighbors.

When darkness came we faced the dilemma of what to do with the trees. Since no one wanted to spend the night there as a watchman, we decided to haul each tree up a steep hill and store them in a garage until the next morning. This we did night after night. After a few weeks the remaining trees looked pretty pitiful.

After Christmas we had to get rid of the leftover trees. I think one of the dads brought a trailer and took the remains to the dump.

None of us were game to repeat the venture the next year.

Scouting was good for us. We learned many things that proved useful in the years ahead. In fact, I'm sure those experiences, along with family camping trips, accounted for my avid interest in the out-of-doors and my summer employment with the Forest Service.

Life is like that. We build on past experiences. This is true spiritually as well. It seems that God has a powerful and providential way to so order our lives that we draw on past experiences to serve him better as the years go by. He is a Master Builder and he continually works in us to shape us into a vessel for his use.

Sometimes we may discount our abilities and experiences. We may belittle ourselves and feel our lives don't add up to much. Not so in God's eyes! He delights in using the foolish things of this life—and our multitude of weaknesses—to mold us into his image.

Our job is to yield our lives to the work of his hands...and to employ all the energy and good sense he inspires within us.

Chapter 7

The Pain of Betrayal

For the most part I had a happy childhood. I got along well with my peers and most of the adults in my life. There were, however, a few exceptions.

One of my first recollections of an unhappy event dates back to the playfield in grade school. The school bully, a tall sixth-grader of unlikeable character, let me have it in the mouth during recess. The blow knocked me to the ground and I recall lying there in pain and humiliation. It hurt to be hit like that, but the pain to my pride was worse.

I was a pipsqueak fourth grader and I knew my chances of getting even with the tyrant fell somewhere between zero and zilch. So I got up, brushed myself off, and went on my way. Sometimes you need to know when to fight, when to go with the flow, and when to flee.

One time, on the sidewalk outside of church, a fellow grade-schooler popped me in the nose for something I had said. I ran to the bathroom with blood running down my face.

I didn't try to even the score but instead made a mental note *not* to invite this kid to my next birthday party.

I've always been a peace-loving person, so I don't have spine-tingling stories of me rolling around on the ground pummeling and being pummeled. Rather than aggravate others with physical abuse I found myself more in the category of a playful tormentor. Sometimes my aggravations earned a negative response. The following story is a case in point.

I was feeling my oats at youth camp one summer and went a bit too far in the teasing department. Consequently, three of my friends felt compelled to execute justice. In spite of my efforts to cling to my pants, they were removed and ceremoniously hoisted up the flagpole. There they flapped in the breeze as a reminder of the biblical injunction, "Whatsoever a man sows, that shall he also reap." (By the way, I wasn't the only one that summer to have high-flying pants.)

When I reached the sensitive age of 12 or 13 I received more than I deserved. One night a group of "friends" ganged up on me in the darkness. They were led by a guy who had endured one too many of my practical jokes.

At a signal from the leader, they suddenly jumped me and knocked me to the ground. Some of them pinned me down while the ringleader cut my hair with shears and then poured glue on my head.

I was helpless to fight back. All I could do was lay there and suffer the ignominy of their meanness. I knew these guys well and they were my friends. Yet that night on the grass I tasted the bitter gall of betrayal.

I remember going home in tears and feeling so very broken inside. My mother rinsed my hair out with glue-cutting solvent and then she trimmed my hair as best she could. Mom and Dad sought to comfort me and assured me it was not the end of the world.

Over time, the emotional wounds of that evening healed. My relationships with the assailants returned to normal. In fact, the ringleader and I eventually had many positive experiences together in high school and college. Yet, in spite of good times we enjoyed, our friendship was never quite the same.

I suspect many of us have been hurt and disappointed by the disloyalty of a friend—someone we thought we could count on, someone we trusted. Even though we might forgive the person and continue the friendship, the memory of betrayal lingers.

In one of his psalms, David writes of a trusted friend who forsook him in a time of trouble. We feel his heart-wrenching anguish in the words, "Even my close friend, whom I trusted, he who shared my bread, has lifted up his heel against me."

I think of the pain Jesus must have felt when his closest friends failed him in his supreme hour of need. When the going got tough, they forsook him and fled.

Wonderfully, there was no sign of personal revenge or getting even on the Lord's part. He absorbed the hurt of betrayal and took it with him to the cross. There he paid the price for all our sins. His love exceeds our failings and covers our guilt.

Human friendships are wonderful and healthy and healing and all the rest...but they can also be the source for our greatest agony—especially when we invest the kind of trust in flesh and blood that belongs only to God. When we place supreme faith in other imperfect persons we will—at some point—suffer disappointment.

Thank God for the One who *never* leaves us nor forsakes us! He is the Friend above all friends, a Companion in all the ups and downs of life. He alone is more loyal and true than any friendship or marriage or partnership or other human relationship. And even though we are disloyal to him and "lift up our heel against him" he remains true to us.

What a Friend we have in Jesus!

Chapter 8

Waxing Eloquent for Fun ℰↄ

What do three teens do when church is boring and the preacher drones on and on? They excuse themselves and find refuge in a Sunday school classroom. At least, this is what we did during those awkward years.

Looking back, I doubt the services were all that boring and I wonder how we were able to escape without parental capture. Yet at times we found our way to the educational wing and one particular room that had a lectern and generous seating. Employing our imaginations, we turned the classroom into a lecture hall and filled it with imagined dignitaries from around the world.

The first speaker rose and went to the front to make the introduction. Each of us took a turn at this role. I might say, "Esteemed guests from far and wide and noted scientists and philosophers from the civilized world, ladies and gentlemen and members of the press, it is my great honor to introduce to you our guest speaker today."

49

Then I would proceed with every adulatory word imaginable to recognize the many achievements and awards of the speaker, taking a good 5 or 7 minutes to properly introduce such an honored and esteemed speaker. The final word would be the announcement of the topic to be addressed by the speaker. This would be the first time the other two teens would learn of the topic, and it would be something really off the wall. For example, I remember one time I was to speak on "The Sleeveless Orange." The "East African Yellow-Bellied Sap Sucker" was another topic I recall.

Applause would then erupt from the third person in the room as the guest speaker rose and made his way to the front. After a minute or so of calming down the audience of two and expressing gratitude for such a magnanimous introduction, he would approach the invisible bank of microphones and begin his 15-20 minute oration.

At times the whole thing got so silly the three of us roared with laughter. The speaker would sometimes have to stop because of a side ache from the hilarity of it all.

When the speaker ended, there would be a standing ovation and wild cheers of appreciation.

Then the third teen would go to the podium and introduce the next speaker of the day. We usually got through two speeches before we had to vacate the room and blend in with the crowd exiting the sanctuary.

As we matured, we developed more innovative activities. For example, at age 16 we formed a dancing group. I am using the term "dancing" very loosely. It was more of a gymnastic free-for-all that displayed perpetual and uncoordinated motion. Four of us young men became known as "The Rah Rah Boys."

To give you an idea of a typical session, come with me to my parent's home on the lower north side of Queen Anne Hill in Seattle, Washington. Mom and Dad are out for the evening and my sister is away elsewhere. My three friends arrive with eager expressions of, "Let's get the show on the road!"

We open the front door and the back door to allow us to exit the kitchen and run around the yard and enter the house again into the living room through the front door. We remind ourselves that the object of this "dance" is to so thoroughly exhaust ourselves that none of us can stand up by the time the song is over.

I go to the hi-fi and put on a record of Benny Goodman and his orchestra playing "Sing, Sing, Sing." It is a hard-driving, fast-moving piece with Gene Krupa at the drums. It runs about 15 minutes. I turn up the volume and suddenly four 16-year-olds are moving every limb in wild abandonment, jumping up and down, spinning, running through the house and yard, yelling and trying desperately to conk ourselves out before the end of the song.

At the end we would be piled on the floor sweating and panting for air. It was excruciating and we never had the strength to perform an encore.

Sometimes we would be driving around Queen Anne Hill and "Sing, Sing, Sing" would come on the radio. Wherever we were, we'd stop the car, get out, and proceed to perform until the music stopped. More than once we attracted a bewildered audience.

I am shaking my head even now as I recall those senseless times of my youth. You ask me why we did this and I must stare blankly at your question. It was just one of those things we did. No reason. Just letting off steam.

One more confession from my youth. Somewhere along the line we got the idea that staging a fight would be fun. In fact, it was fun, but after doing it a few times we went on to something else.

Picture yourself sitting with your spouse or family around the table or in the living room. The window is clear of shades and you can see outside onto the lawn. A young man is walking along the sidewalk. Suddenly a car screeches to a halt and three guys jump out and race toward the lone pedestrian. He runs onto the lawn screaming for help while the others tackle him and feign a barrage of slugs and kicks. You are glued to the window, or perhaps calling the police.

As quickly as it began the onslaught is over and the attackers jump in the car and race away. The victim lies on the grass groaning. You come closer to see what aid you might offer. As you bend over, the "wounded" teen jumps up and says, "Oh, I feel much better. Thank you for your concern," and then races down the block and around the corner where the car is waiting.

Pretty stupid, huh? But such were the things that occupied the lives of a few high school boys in the mid '50s.

Why do I tell you these things? I guess because you cannot always foretell what may become of an awkward, rambunctious, and fun-loving teen. One of us became a nuclear scientist; another, an effective junior high school teacher; another, a leader in charitable work; and another, a minister of the gospel.

I am also reminded of the wisdom of our parents who gave us enough freedom to express ourselves, while at the same time making sure our church surrounded us with strong youth leaders, programs like Boy Scouts, and advisors who provided wholesome activities. We may have tested the boundaries and did things that embarrassed our parents, but through it all there was a loving atmosphere at home and church that kept us from veering off into serious crime or lasting regret.

As children of our heavenly Father, I marvel at his patience with us. We may do things and say things that reveal immaturity. We may cause our guardian angels to shake their heads. But through it all, we are growing in the grace and knowledge of our Lord Jesus Christ.

Perhaps it is also good to recall some of our youthful antics as a way to nudge ourselves away from being too serious and too stilted in our older years. While keeping an eye on protocol and suitability, we might do well to have some fun along the way.

Chapter 9

Great Falls

I don't recall my first fall. It surely happened when I was a toddler learning to walk. I must have tumbled plenty of times during those months. But once I was able to stand and walk solidly, my falls diminished significantly.

Then came the falls that remain etched in my memory. The first that comes to mind occurred when I was five or six years old. We had a detached garage at the rear of our house. It had a flat roof and periodically I had to climb a ladder to go up there to retrieve a ball or something. I think it was a Saturday when several neighborhood kids were playing in our backyard. Somehow the conversation turned to parachutes and umbrellas, and I made the claim that I could jump off the garage roof with an umbrella and glide safely to the ground.

Taunted by dares and double-dares, and maybe even a double-dog-dare-you challenge, I retrieved an umbrella from the house and climbed the ladder to the roof. With every eye pinned on me I opened the umbrella, stepped to the edge of the roof, and plunged toward the earth. The umbrella turned inside out and I landed with a thud. Fortunately, I suffered only the guffaws from my friends.

Years later, in high school, I spent time at a local roller-skating rink. On one occasion our church youth group rented the rink for an evening social. Other church groups were invited to make the occasion feasible. Since I was known by management to be a fairly good skater, I was asked to assist with monitoring the activity. I'd help fallen skaters get back on their feet and when the music stopped, I'd help clear the floor so the next event could begin (couples only, ladies only, etc.). After clearing the floor, I was the only skater out there, zooming by in front of the crowd as a person of importance (in my eyes).

Why not flip around and skate backwards like I frequently did, I asked myself. So I spun around. However, in the process, I got my feet tangled and down I went, smashing my head on the wooden floor and skidding on my back for several yards. At least 99.9 percent of the skaters witnessed my fall. I got up, acting like it was nothing at all, and skated over to an exit to take a seat. There I gathered my thoughts, inventoried my injuries, and massaged my pride. It was, without doubt, one of my great falls.

Another notable fall occurred during my college years. I was president of a student organization called Fireside Fellowship. Each Sunday night 250 or so students met for singing, prayer, and an inspirational talk. At the beginning of the school year, the officers met to plan future programs and social events. One year we went to Lake Goodwin near Everett, Washington. Saturday afternoon was reserved for recreation. Someone brought a ski boat, so several of us took turns skimming across the lake on water skis.

I started from the dock with two skis and the boat pulled me around for maybe 5 minutes and then brought me back around by the dock where I dropped one ski. Then we headed out for another run. This time when the driver came back toward the dock I leaned hard against the rope, crossed the wake, and swung close to the dock in a show of skill. Just as I was about to zoom by the onlookers, I hit the ski I had dropped off during my previous run.

I did a complete summersault and landed in a violent splash that surely evoked a chorus of gasps from the dock. I surfaced okay and collected the two floating skis and paddled my way to the dock with wounded pride. That was a fall I have been unable to forget.

Other falls come to mind as I dwell on this topic. I have fallen downstairs and even upstairs. I've fallen on mountain trails, on the fields and courts of competition, off chairs and ladders, and in refined and dignified settings. Most of these falls, it seems, occurred in the presence of others. And most of them revealed a careless attitude, impatience, or a bit of pride. In most cases, I deserved what I got.

One of the more recent falls occurred just a few years ago in Leavenworth. It was winter and I had come over to our mountain home to do some work. Now I was on my way back to Edmonds where Sandy was waiting for me to arrive in time to go to church. I stopped at the gas station on the west edge of town to top off the tank and get some coffee. It was snowing as I pulled under the roofed part of the station next to an island with two gas pumps.

Thinking nothing of it, I opened the door and dropped down from the cab of the pickup to the frozen cement. Unfortunately,

I landed on a clear sheet of ice and went sprawling, smashing my left elbow and shoulder on the ground. It happened instantly and I could easily have struck my head on the curb of the island, causing serious injury or perhaps death.

I got to my knees and assessed my injuries. A station attendant (who was tossing salt on another section of cement) hurried to my aid. I waited a minute before rising and then slowly got to my feet. The manager came out looking distraught. She offered free aspirin and water and anything else I needed.

After receiving a cup of hot coffee and a few donuts, I climbed back in the truck and eased out on the highway for the trip over the snowy pass to Edmonds.

As I drove, I considered what had just happened to me.

First, the ice patch was entirely unexpected. I knew the roadway was icy, but I never considered for a moment that I would run into ice under the canopy of the station. I was oblivious to the danger, thinking only of gas for the truck and food for my stomach.

Second, my fall happened suddenly. No warning, no time to grab something—just 250 pounds of human mass smashing to the ground like a giant fir tree falling in the forest.

Third, it hurt! My elbow and shoulder ached and my head throbbed the rest of the day.

All of this, including the falls mentioned earlier, remind and instruct me about the dangers of temptation and the effects of sin. Sometimes, when we least expect it, our enemy crafts a sheet of ice in our path. As we go merrily along, thinking about our appetites, we step unknowingly onto his icy trap and sprawl headlong to the ground. It can happen so suddenly, so swiftly, that given a careless attitude, we are unable to stop the fall. How discomforting to acknowledge our weakness and our failure to walk uprightly in the Lord. How it hurts when we fall into sin.

The Bible is full of failures and falls. Consider Adam and Eve in the Garden, David and Bathsheba, and Peter's denial—to mention a few.

Jesus warns us repeatedly to watch where we're going, to keep our eyes open, and to be alert. He tells us to step in his steps and to follow his leading.

Paul warned the Corinthians to take heed lest they fall. The same caution applies to us whether we are jumping from the heights of ignorance with the faulty parachutes of human ingenuity and misplaced confidence; whether we are thinking more highly of ourselves than we ought to think as we skate through life; whether we are carelessly skimming across the waters of self-sufficiency; or whether we are stepping carelessly on the slippery surfaces of personal desire.

So let my careless tumbles warn and instruct you today. Don't trust in human efforts to land softly when you jump into wrongdoing. Rather than skating backwards to proudly adore past achievements and accomplishments, keep your eyes on the Lord. Watch for obstacles ahead of you by acting wisely and with humility. And make sure you are on solid ground with good traction. Remember, your crafty and deceitful enemy is always looking for ways to bring you down.

Finally, remember that, should you fall, the Lord is faithful and just and will forgive you and wash away your guilt. He is always there to take your hand and lift you up and set your feet on solid ground.

Chapter 10

Episodes of Help

I hate to ask for help. There's just something about having to admit that I can't solve a problem or fix something myself. It's humbling to say "Help."

It is especially agonizing when we occupy a position of authority and find ourselves calling for assistance from someone under our supervision. A doctor doesn't seek medical help from a patient. A teacher doesn't ask a student help in a personal matter. Nor does a Forest Service employee ask "a member of the public" to help him out of a jam. Or does he?

During the summer I worked as a Forest Service Patrolman in the back country in the Snoqualmie National Forest, I occasionally cut wood for campers at the Taylor River Campground. Several trees had been felled the previous year and I was supposed to cut them into rounds and then split them into usable chunks for campfires.

The chainsaw I was using was high pitched and extra loud. My ears began to ring and so I stopped and wadded up two pieces of toilet paper and jammed them into my ears. Then I proceeded cutting the wood. I worked for a couple of hours and put the saw back in the truck. When I reached up to pull the wadded paper out of my ears, I couldn't find the plugs. The paper had worked itself well into both ears.

And so, dressed in my Forest Service attire and covered with woodchips and sweat, I went to one of the camp spots and asked if someone had a pair of tweezers and could help me get the paper out of my ears. I remember sitting on a log while an older man carefully dug into my ear to locate and remove the wads of paper. I felt pretty wimpy about the whole thing.

Years later, while volunteering at the Granite Mountain Lookout Station, I managed to get a good-sized splinter implanted in my right hand. I didn't have tweezers, so I tried to dig it out with a needle. That failed and so I waited for a visitor to show up. Later that day two men arrived and when they climbed the steps and entered the lookout, I asked "Do either of you have a pair of tweezers?" One did and very kindly "operated" on my hand to remove the splinter. Again, I felt stupid standing there receiving help from a stranger.

One of the more memorable episodes occurred when I was in college. A friend of mine, Deane, lived a block away from campus and became addicted to bodybuilding workouts. He converted half of their detached two-car garage into a gym with punching bag, barbells, and other muscle-building tools.

Occasionally I would join him and a couple other friends who began hanging out there. I never did get to the place where I wanted to show off my muscles, mostly because I never really had anything worth displaying!

The garage was above the level of the house and a set of stairs led down to the kitchen door. The door to the "gym" was usually unlocked, so any of us could drop by and work out by ourselves if we wanted.

I don't recall the day of the week nor the time, but when I arrived, Deane was gone. Undeterred, I opened the large door and started a mild workout routine. When it came time for the bench press, I set the bar on the holders above the bench and loaded the weights on each end. Then I laid down on the bench, took hold of the bar above me, and grunted the weights into the air.

I knew almost immediately that I had put too many pounds on the bar. I also knew that I should have a spotter there to help me get the bar back on the holders if I could not make that last upward thrust.

I did a couple of presses and then the unthinkable happened. I simply could not lift the heavy bar back onto the holders. So I lay there helplessly squashed beneath the 250 pound (or whatever it was) bar. The only thing I could think to do was to call out for help.

Deane's mother was a delicate woman and always, it seemed to me, impeccably dressed. Apparently she was working in the kitchen and heard my hollering. She came out, climbed the stairs, and entered the garage. Together, we managed to lift the bar onto the holders and set me free.

Although I was mortified by having to ask Deane's mother for help, I was glad she was within earshot. I could still be there pinned to the bench!

It's hard for some of us to ask for help. We have to be pretty desperate.

One time Sandy and I drove up to Vancouver, B.C. to visit our daughter who was attending seminary. That afternoon, the three of us went out for a drive and I said, "Hey, let's go find the church where I preached several years ago. I'm pretty sure I can drive straight to it."

So I continued in what I thought was the correct direction. As we drove on and on, the volume of advice mounted, "Why don't you stop and ask directions?" "Let's get a map." "Why don't we check the Yellow Pages?"

For three hours I drove around, believing with all my heart I could locate the church by the seat of my pants. Asking for directions was not an option.

By the time I gave up and we found our way back to my daughter's apartment, my stature as a navigator had plummeted to a new low. The term "annoyance" does not even come close to how my companions felt.

I suppose the idea of asking for God's help is harder for some of us than others. Perhaps it's a pride thing, or maybe a self-help determination that drives us forward. Sometimes we have to get ourselves into a fix before we will break down and ask the Lord for help. How the angels must shake their heads.

As a father of four, I have known the sheer joy of having one of my kids come to me with a problem, or otherwise seek my help. It made me feel good to provide soothing words, a kiss on a sore, a comforting hug, or any of a hundred other remedies. If I delight in helping my children, how much more does God our Father yearn to hear our calls for help?

It may be humbling to admit we need help, but that is exactly what our Father desires of us. It may work somewhat the same way with each other. Asking is not a sign of weakness, but an admission that we are human and willing to elevate others by seeking their assistance.

Episodes of Help

Some people, of course, will turn a deaf ear to our requests. They are lost in their own selfish worlds. But there are others, perhaps most, who will gladly lend a helping hand. As Solomon might have written, "There is a time to ask for help and a time to help others."

Chapter 11

Living With
Pests

Anyone who wants to camp out had better be ready for pests. You can expect ants, mosquitos, gnats, bees, flies, and other pesky irritants. There's a whole industry dedicated to ward off these pests and you best stock up on such deterrents before heading for the woods.

Some people seem to attract more of these pests than others. I am one of those magnets. Over the years I have been attacked, bitten, stung, chewed on, and otherwise pestered by zillions of these creatures.

One of the more painful memories dates back to the mid-1980s when my son, Jonathan, and I loaded up our inflatable boat for a trip to a desolate beach on Dabob Bay in the upper section of Hood Canal. I had been there by floatplane several times and now we wanted to take our gear and camp there for two or three days. Since we were not packing the stuff on our backs, we loaded up with extra clothes, cookware, tent, sleeping bags, stove, fishing gear, and a significant amount of food.

We drove to the little marina on Quilcene Bay where we readied the 14-foot boat for the trip. This was going to be a luxurious camping experience. Little did we know at the time that the most vivid memory would make us wince for years to come.

We set the outboard motor in place, hooked up the gas, and started off for the larger bay to the east. Since we were loaded down with gear, the boat refused to plane. We had to content ourselves with slow moving water-plowing. By the time we reached our destination on the other bay, the sun was sinking behind the Olympic Mountains to the west. We had to hustle to set up camp before darkness swallowed us.

It was high tide and the area of beach we had planned to occupy was underwater. There was, however, a grassy shelf of land up from the beach and so we hauled everything there, including the motor. Our plan was to carry the boat up above the high-water mark where it would be safe.

Once we got things in place, we proceeded to spread out a tarp and open the sleeping bags. It was then we discovered a colony of unhappy ants. No, that is incorrect. It was not one colony but a colony of colonies. We had quite innocently stumbled into the largest infestation of big black ants I have ever seen. They were everywhere—scurrying through our stuff, crawling up our legs, covering our hands when we tried to pick something up.

Clearly we could not stay there. We decided to haul the boat back down to the water and fill it with a few necessities for the night. We left everything else behind, including the motor. We rowed out a hundred yards from shore, dropped our little anchor, and prepared to ride out the night. Unfortunately, a small army of ants occupied the boat with us and it took several minutes to complete a find and destroy mission.

The water was calm and darkness fell upon us as we stretched out on the bottom of the inflatable. It would have been fairly comfortable for one person, but two bodies significantly exceeded the floor space. We dozed on and off until we both woke to the realization that the wind was blowing and the boat rocking. We looked out and saw whitecaps glistening in the moonlight.

For the rest of the night we contemplated what would happen if the anchor pulled loose and we drifted out beyond the mouth of the bay. Then an even more uncomfortable thought came to mind. What if one of the large sea lions that frequent these waters decided to pop out of the water and land on top of us? We both had seen similar things happen by the ferry docks when seals and sea lions lumbered onto floats to rest.

That did it. We were wide-eyed until the first glimmer of light. We rowed to the shore and loaded all our ant-covered gear for the ride back to Quilcene Bay.

A few ants on a camping trip can be handled easily. Having a tent can also help keep the little pests at bay. But when you encounter a horde of unhappy ants, it's time to find the nearest motel.

On another occasion, Jonathan and I hiked into the Enchantment Lakes, near where we now live in Icicle Canyon. This is a tough climb and you've got to be prepared for any number of surprises. When we got well into the Enchantments, we took a side trail up and over a ridge and into what is known as the Rat Creek Basin. This is a remote area and the reports of privacy and great fishing drew us there.

We made it in time to set up camp and prepare dinner. The next morning we rose to discover that our arrival coincided with a "gnat hatch." There were hordes of these little pests all around us. They are very small—like tiny flies—yet they can bite. They travel in swarms so it is not a matter of smacking one that happens to land on your face. They engulf your entire head.

We brought beekeeper hoods and promptly put them on so we could breathe without sucking in a swarm of gnats. We covered any exposed flesh with repellant. All that day and the next we battled these little pests. When we'd lift up our hood to put a spoon of food in our mouths, we'd ingest a few gnats as well. We fished and tried to go about our day enjoying the scenery and our time together. You can imagine our relief when a batch of dragonflies hatched and ate the gnats.

A third memory brings us back to Shield Lake a few years later. This time I was with a co-worker who had not been on an overnight hike. Remembering the gnat fiasco, we stocked up with an ample supply of deterrent and screening. I did not tell him what we might encounter lest he decide to stay home.

However, when we arrived there was not a gnat in sight. The weather was clear and the fish were biting. It was the perfect trip, except for one thing—ravenous mosquitos. When I tell you that we spent a good part of our three days and nights at Shield Lake inside the tent, you will understand the enormity of our plight. We were, to those kamikazes, mortal enemies.

It didn't seem to matter what cream or spray we used or how many mosquitos we slapped into oblivion; they just kept coming. They had a thirst for every drop of blood coursing through our veins.

We'd sit in the tent and watch the long-nosed blood suckers stick their beaks right through the screening. There might be 20 or more all greedily trying to get through the mesh at once. We'd take our fingers and thumbs and flick them away, hoping to bust a few noses in the process. It was man against mosquito with both opponents—insect and human—using all the skills acquired beforehand for such battles.

Except for a few hours in the late morning and afternoon, we lived in the tent. We had our packs with us to reduce the need to leave our place of safety. When evening approached, the mosquitos ratcheted up their offensive.

The worst part came when one of us had to leave the tent to make the inevitable trip to a nearby tree. The remaining person would quickly open and close the flap for the exit, and then repeat the rapid action upon the person's return. Then it would be hunt and kill any unfortunate pest that happened to make it into the tent.

You don't have to go on a camping trip to encounter pests. There are plenty of them closer to home. In fact, as I type this on a lanai here in Palm Desert, I have a fly swatter at hand to protect myself from one particular pesky fly.

Let's leave the world of insects and consider the other kinds of irritants that sometimes plague our existence. Like the three examples above, these pesky things are often small and incessant.

There are people in our lives that we might consider pesky, but I am thinking today of other irritants we may encounter along the way, such as temptations that needle us to speak unkindly or to ignore a person in need. Sometimes the evil one sticks with us like the fly buzzing around my head right now.

It would be nice if we could sail through life enjoying the many blessings of God without interference. But God has not ordained it so. Like insects on a camping trip, we must deal with spiritual pests along life's road.

This means clothing ourselves with the protective gear of God's righteousness. It means applying an ample dosage of the balm of Gilead. It also means equipping ourselves with the Sword of the Spirit which is the Word of God.

In this world we will never be pest-free; irritations abound. But praise God, for "in all these things we are more than conquerors through him who loved us."

Chapter 12

When Prince
Went Berserk

For two years we lived in a cottage on the outskirts of Ellensburg, Washington. I was working on my Masters at Central Washington University and Sandy was teaching school. Our wood-heated little home was situated on a farm where our friends, Yvonne and Gene, raised children, sweet corn, and cattle. It was a good time in our lives.

Our landlords also had two horses: Sweena and Prince. I think they were Arabians and not more than a few years old. Sweena was gentle and the landlord's daughter rode her across the acreage—both ponytails flying in the wind. The other horse had never had a rider on his back. He was a frisky sort and liked to run and snort and show off.

My work at the university centered on experimental psychology with an emphasis on personal counseling. Besides taking classes and practicums, I helped as an assistant within the department. This meant I taught introductory psych classes to underclassmen and worked with fellow grad students in various ways. The professors were busy conducting experiments and

73

writing scholarly papers, so I did more of their work than I should have been doing.

During this time, the conditioning techniques of behaviorism (B.F. Skinner) drove the experimental emphasis at the university. We learned how behavior can be altered incrementally through positive rewards for desired outcomes. The example of Pavlov's salivating dog served as our model.

A typical application might be helping a person overcome a phobia by taking them through a series of small steps whereby they would experience increasing exposure to the source of their fears, rewarding them with affirming words or other positives at each tiny indication of success. Eventually they would be conditioned to comfortably accept what had frightened them before.

I worked with laboratory rats as well as college freshmen. The former were more controllable, though I did get bit once handling one of the larger rodents. My thesis involved two groups of "volunteers" from my Introduction to Psychology classes—one as the control group and the other as the unwitting experimental group. I called my effort, "The Reduction of Cognitive Dissonance During the Performance of a Dull Task." Though statistically significant, the results were never published.

There were only six students going through the experimental program in counseling so we became well acquainted. Bill was an outdoor kind of guy and we began fishing and hiking together.

One day I told him about Sweena and Prince and asked whether he'd like to help me apply behavioral techniques to breaking the horse that had never been ridden. He was all for it and so I talked to Gene that evening and he said, "Go for it."

When Prince Went Berserk

Bill and I laid out a simple plan with an emphasis on gentleness, patience, and consistency. Using oats for bait, I got Prince into the corral and we began to make friends with the animal. Since I lived onsite, it fell on me to do most of the daily training.

I would stand in the corral with a chunk of apple and reward Prince for coming to me. I'd talk slow and easy to him and pat his neck. One day I held a halter near him and even rubbed it on his neck. A day or two later he was wearing the halter.

Bill and I took turns leading Prince around the corral and got to the point where we could stand in the middle and cause him to run around the edges while one of us held the rope.

In like manner we were able to position the bridle and lay a blanket on his back. Then the saddle, then the saddle with the cinch fastened. I added some weight by pulling down on the saddle horn. Weeks went by as we worked with Prince, following each advance with words of affirmation and a treat.

The day came when I stepped into the stirrup and slowly lifted my leg over the horse. He shuddered and I readied myself for flight. He did buck a few times, but not violently. Then he moved around the corral nervously and I just let him have his way.

A few days later we opened the gate and I rode Prince into the pasture. That was the beginning of many rides, not only at the farm, but also up Manastash Ridge nearby.

Gene had a small herd of cattle and I helped move them a few miles on county roads to a range area in Robinson Canyon. On that day I played cowboy, and Prince did his job like a pro.

In all the time I rode Prince I was never bucked off or feared for my safety...except for that one incident on the Pacific Coast Trail.

Gene was generous with the horses and let Bill and me ride anytime we wanted. Bill would ride Sweena and I'd take Prince. As our horsemanship skills increased, we expanded our horizons for longer rides. I asked Gene if we could take the horses on a three-day trail ride on the Pacific Coast Trail (PCT) from Stampede Pass to Snoqualmie Pass. He agreed. This was not a great distance, but long enough to allow for a leisurely ride with frequent stops along the way.

We arranged with one of our profs to take us to the starting point and then to pick us up in three days at Snoqualmie Pass. He had a hefty pickup truck and we rented a horse trailer to haul Sweena and Prince. We packed our gear and acquired needed items, such as horse-fly oil and a modest supply of oats. We were counting on grass for feed.

The day arrived and we loaded the horses and drove onto Interstate 90 for the 45-minute drive to the Stampede Pass turn-off. None of us had been to that pass before and were unaware of how steep and rocky the access road was. About half way up, the tires of the pickup started to spin and our progress ceased. We could neither back up nor go forward. So we got out, blocked the tires, and unloaded the horses on the steep slope.

With a lighter load, the truck made it to a turnaround spot and prof was able to get back down the hill.

We saddled the horses and continued our trip to the trail. What a thrill to actually set out on the famous Pacific Coast Trail with Prince and Sweena! How exciting to enjoy the scenery from the lofty heights of the saddles! It was as though all our efforts at "horse conditioning" were paying off in grand style.

The first night on the trail was horrible. The horse flies and mosquitoes swarmed around us, and the horses nearly went mad. The oil and sprays we brought provided only temporary relief. And even though we found refuge in our tent, Bill and I kept going out to the horses to try and calm them. It was a long, sleepless night and we quickly concluded that neither we nor the horses could stand another night of such distress. We decided to leave at daybreak and go all the way to Snoqualmie Pass.

The next day, sometime before noon, we were riding along once more enjoying the experience of having horses carry us. We could scan the scenery without watching our feet and feeling the weight of a pack. A small contingent of horseflies accompanied us, but we seemed to be free of serious hindrance.

We came to a narrow section of trail and I noted how sharply the side of the mountain fell away from us to the right. It was then, at that precise moment, that one of those big, fat, pesky flies entered Prince's ear.

Instantly, the horse went berserk and bolted off the trail down the slope. I had the presence of mind to roll off his back and retain a grip on the reigns. He pulled me a ways, and then swung around to face the upside of the mountain. Had I let go, he would probably still be running today. Blood poured from a gash above my left eye.

God be praised, there were no broken bones of horse or man. We made it back to the trail and Bill doctored my wound. It didn't require stitches, though I still have a faint scar near my eyebrow.

We reached Snoqualmie Pass late in the afternoon and called prof to come and get us a day early. While waiting, we laid in the shade and counted our blessings. As for the berserky behavior of Prince on the trail, we decided that there was something seriously lacking in the doctrines of behavioral conditioning.

Of the various lessons we learned from our trail-riding experience on the PCT, a few are worth noting—especially those with spiritual application.

Life is a trail ride, a combination of pesky irritants and awesome scenery. We encounter things or people that get under our skin and make life miserable. These we learn to endure while finding ways to apply the calming balm of kindness. Eventually the "night" of distress departs and we can look out over the landscape of life and enjoy the handiwork of God. The long sleepless nights perform their purposes and the sunshine of a new day brings fresh illumination and wonder.

Sometimes things suddenly occur out of the blue and knock us off the trail. All we can do is hang on and hope the downward drag will cease. Amazingly, by God's grace it does and we again find the trail and continue on.

There is more to life than mechanistic outcomes of behavioral conditioning. We are souls with hopes and dreams and eternal destinies. God rules over us all and in his Son, Jesus Christ, we are saved from our sins and cleansed of all guilt. We behold beauty and feel love. We are children of God, born to live in fellowship with him. The realities of spiritual life transcend physical existence.

There is a verse in the Psalms about the folly of trusting in horses. How true, whether the horse is a four-legged animal, a behavioral scheme, or any other device or creed. We are pilgrims bound for the Promised Land and our only hope is found in Jesus' blood and righteousness.

The apostle Paul learned that he was not always able to do the right things he wanted to do, but sometimes did the opposite. A sudden blast of temptation when we least expect it can also cause us failure. No matter how conditioned and disciplined we are to living steady, consistent lives, we can taste the dirt of disobedience without warning.

Thank God for his unlimited and enduring grace! When we confess our bolts from the trail, he is faithful to forgive us and cleanse us from our unrighteousness, and set our feet back on the Upward Way.

Chapter 13

First Aid in the Wilderness

I once took a mountain first aid course to get better equipped to handle medical emergencies in the back country. A dozen of us met weekly for classroom lectures and real-life training. We practiced our life-saving techniques on each other and bandaged one another for a score of imaginary wounds.

We would break into teams of two or three and another one or two would be positioned outside or someplace inside as victims. Then, pretending to be out hiking, we'd come upon these victims and go through the process of diagnosis and immediate treatment and rescue. We dealt with severe bleeding, broken bones, shock, seizure, hypothermia, and dehydration. I remember one rainy night when we stumbled upon three "victims" that had supposedly fallen down a hill and had assorted injuries.

On another occasion, a person might be suffering an epileptic seizure. Once I was the "victim" and had to fake a broken back. Being somewhat on the hefty side, it was interesting to hear the grunts and groans of my colleagues as they tried to gingerly lift me onto a make-shift stretcher.

We learned about first aid materials and the minimum amount of items we should always carry with us on the trail. Each of us developed our own kit of cloth bandages, sterile pads, antiseptic solutions, and other necessary aids. We were exhorted never to set foot on a trail without our packet of life-saving materials.

The "final exam" consisted of an outdoor, night-time sequence of medical emergencies in a "wilderness setting" (Camp Long in West Seattle). Victims were planted here and there and we, in groups of three, had to move through a series of encounters, allowing only so much time with each scenario. A "grader" accompanied us to record our successes and failures. Then we had a debriefing session to go over the evening.

I suppose the main reason I took the course was to prepare me for medical emergencies involving myself and my hiking companions. However, as the weeks progressed, I developed a larger view of wilderness readiness. I began to understand that my training was not just for me and my friends, but for anyone I might come across on the trail.

In fact, we were exhorted with, "How would you feel coming upon an injured hiker miles from the road and not having the slightest idea how to help? You need to be prepared to help others who may die without your assistance."

I had never really considered that before. My concern had always been myself and my family and friends. Even at that, I had been poorly prepared with knowledge, skill, and equipment. My Boy Scout merit badge in first aid and CPR had long been forgotten.

The course was a wake-up call for me to think about strangers on the trail...and to be ready to help them in a crisis.

You can see the obvious application to our spiritual lives. It is so easy to lock into a pattern of concern that centers solely on personal and family needs, and a short list of our closest friends. We pray for and care for each other and go about our journey as though we would never encounter a wounded soul on the Samaritan Road.

Yet, our preparation as "life savers" is meant for strangers as well as family and friends. We are to equip ourselves to face whatever and whoever we find in the wilderness of this world. We are to shoulder the equipment of mercy, the salve of compassion, the bandages of grace, the splints of encouragement, the blanket of understanding, the water of life, the fire of hope, the sacred plasma of forgiveness...we are to carry all of these with us, always ready to stop and minister to casualties we encounter along the way.

The wilderness settings we encounter are not confined to the backcountry. I lived on Manhattan Island for a year and found myself confronting derelicts lying here and there on the sidewalk. At first I felt obligated to minister in some way to each one of them, but soon found this to be impossible. I became somewhat hardened at the sight of bums on the street. It troubled me to lose a degree of compassion. Here I was studying at seminary to be a minister of God while stepping over needy souls on the seminary's porch.

Once, in Seattle, I was in the midst of rush-hour foot traffic, making my way over a pedestrian bridge to catch a ferry to Bainbridge Island. Attorneys, secretaries, executives, and others jostled to make it in time before the ferry left. About half way there, I came upon a man lying on the side of the walkway.

Hundreds of hurried people stepped around him to reach their destination. I stopped momentarily to look closely at the man. He was passed out or dead, I couldn't tell. He was disheveled and pitiful. I felt an impulse to do something, but I couldn't think of what to do, so I hurried along with the rest of the crowd toward the ferry.

That scene haunts me to this day. Would that I had got down on my knees and placed my hand on his head and prayed for God to be merciful to this man and to deliver him from the bondage of alcohol or whatever it was that imprisoned him. Would that I had bent to his ear and spoken words of life and hope and love from God our Father. Would that I had used my cell phone to call for an ambulance.

First aid in the wilderness—that's what we're called to provide. May the Lord give us strength, wisdom, and compelling compassion to reach out to those who are lost or hurt on the pathways of life.

> *Lead me, dear Lord, and let me be,*
> *Ready to stop and stoop with Thee;*
> *To help the ones beside the road,*
> *Ignored by passersby busy and cold.*
> *Grant me the salve of kindly deed,*
> *The touch of healing and words that heed,*
> *The truth of God for every soul:*
> *"I can make the wounded whole."*
>
> —GRS

Chapter 14

The Dingford Creek Fire

I spent the summer of '58 as a patrolman for the U.S. Forest Service in the backcountry at a place called Camp Brown. The small cabin was located at the confluence of two rivers in the Cascade Mountains: Taylor River and the Middle Fork of the Snoqualmie. I was a sophomore at Seattle Pacific College and my partner attended Whitworth College in Spokane.

One day when Merlin was in town taking some time off, I received a call on the radio. A lightning-caused fire had been spotted by an airline pilot in the Dingford Creek area of the Middle Fork drainage. The ranger wanted me to get up there as a first responder.

He said there were two members of the trail crew working on the Taylor River Campground and told me to take them with me. He gave me the approximate location on a sectional map, saying that I'd have to do some cross-country climbing up a mountain. Others would be joining us as soon a team could be mobilized.

I grabbed my fire-fighting pack and headed to the campground for the two workers. They had emergency fire-fighting packs in their truck so we were ready to go. We drove up the bumpy gravel road along the Middle Fork River until we came to the Dingford Creek trailhead.

When we reached the section marker identified on the trail, we knew it was time to head into the brush. We stacked a few rocks to identify our course and then started up the mountain toward the fire. Because of the tall trees and undergrowth, we couldn't see smoke. Nor could we smell it or hear crackling fire. We just headed up the steep slope, pretty sure we were going in the right direction.

A mile or so later we caught a whiff of smoke and knew we were heading the right way. Then we came to a gigantic slab of granite that was partially covered with moss. It lay in our path and we decided to gingerly make our way up and across it. At the bottom of the slab was a vertical drop of at least a hundred feet.

One of the trail workers began several feet above me so we were both on the rock at the same time. He lost his grip and started to slide down, hitting me and breaking my hold. In God's great mercy, a fallen tree lay across the slab below us and when we plowed into it, we stopped sliding.

With even more care, we continued up the rock with our heavy packs and made the top successfully. I think it is safe to say that the fallen tree on the side of that slab saved both our lives that day.

We finally reached the fire and it was burning strong. At that point, I'm guessing it was about 20 acres and expanding slowly up the mountain. We were not hampered with wind.

The Dingford Creek Fire

My two companions began digging a line along the base of the fire to stop the blaze from creeping downward, while I tried to walk the edge to see how far and fast the fire was moving up the slope. I radioed the ranger with my observations and he told me some loggers were on their way. A fire crew was assembling from various locations and would be coming toward evening. Supplies would be air-dropped by parachute.

Three loggers arrived and I recall one of them wore leather slippers instead of his logging boots. They went to the upside of the fire and got a fire line going well above the flames and thick smoke.

I had met these men before because one of my jobs was to monitor the small logging operations in accordance with weather conditions. When the temperature rose high enough and the humidity dropped far enough, the loggers had to shut down for the day. So I would go to their work sites and spin a humidity-gauge and read the results with them standing there looking over my shoulder. I forget what the shut-down number was, but if it hit that number or below, I had to tell them to pack it in for the day. As you can imagine, I was not a very popular guy on those occasions.

So now these loggers where right there with me, working to save the forest that provided their livelihood.

A single-engine airplane came later in the day to drop a water pump, hose, tools, tents, sleeping bags, and hot meals for us. Unfortunately, the container with the food got hung up high in a tree. The logger with the slippers grabbed a double-bladed ax and walked over to this giant Douglas fir and started whacking away. He was a sight to behold, and soon he had the tree on the ground. The warm food tasted mighty good!

Later, another guy and I constructed a dam out of plastic tarp to trap water from a small creek a hundred yards from the fire line. We set up the pump and strung hose over to the fire. It took around 20 minutes for the dam to fill. The guy at the dam would then start the pump and water would rush through the hose to where I was standing with the nozzle. I would have about 5 minutes of water before the pump shut off and the dam would fill again.

It was almost dark when the fire crew arrived and they got right to work. Before long they had a fire line around the fire and were separating burning pieces within the line. That night the pump operator and I pitched a tent on a small level patch of ground 50 or so feet from the fire line. We were both filthy and exhausted when we hit the sack.

Around 2 a.m. we were both awakened by the sound of a crashing tree that had fallen across the fire line and within a few feet of our tent. The burning tree sent sparks in every direction and we wasted no time getting out of bed and attacking the "spot fires" created by the fallen tree. Next to sliding down the granite slab on the way up the mountain, this was the most frightening moment for me.

We worked all the next day with the water and hose, trying to put out fires inside the line. The ground was covered with 10 or more inches of dry duff—the accumulation of needles and cones and bits of wood since whenever the last fire came through. Consequently, the fire fighters had to dig down below the duff to get to the earth to make a workable fire line.

For my part, I had to stick the nozzle down into the smoldering duff to put out the "underground" fire that was creeping along. When the water hit the smoldering fire under the duff the substance "exploded" in my face. You can imagine what I looked like after a few minutes.

The next day the ranger called me on the radio and said, "George, come on out of there. You've been up there long enough." I remonstrated a bit, but not strongly. Fact is, I was tuckered out.

When I finally made it to the trailhead, a few guys were there handling the staging and communication center. They both looked at me and shook their heads with unbelief. I was covered with grime from head to foot.

When I got back to the cabin it took two or three showers to get clean. By the way, these showers consisted of heating water on the stove, carrying the two pails out back, and pouring the warm water over myself. It was a tedious process but it sure felt good to be clean again.

Those few days as a fire fighter on the side of that mountain was one of the highlights of the summer, but not one I'd like to repeat. Ever since then I've felt keen admiration and respect for those who do this sort of thing for a living. It is dangerous, demanding, and exhausting.

As I think back on that experience, several lessons and applications emerge. First, people come together to face a common foe. Those loggers who had groused about this "19-year-old kid" shutting down their operation fought right alongside of me to stop the spread of a fire. We became friends on the fire line. Sometimes it takes a crisis to bring people together.

Second, people are willing to risk their lives for a good cause. I think of fire and police professionals and the military who put themselves in harm's way to preserve and protect those who are vulnerable and endangered. Every day, these heroes are ready to die in service to others.

Third, helping others can be a dirty job. The religious leaders walked past the man lying beside the road because they had more important things to do...and they didn't want to dirty their hands. The Good Samaritan stopped, rolled up his sleeves and got involved. Are there people in your life who could use a helping hand?

Fourth, fire can be frightening. It is destructive and difficult to subdue. The Bible uses the imagery of fire to describe eternal suffering for those who reject God in this life. Hell is a lake of fire.

Fifth, many forest fires are started by one streak of lightning. A single match can also set a forest ablaze. The Bible describes the tongue as a fire that can harm and destroy. It counsels us to watch our words lest they cause destruction through gossip, anger, or lies.

The Forest Service is fond of saying, "Only You Can Prevent Forest Fires." That is certainly true when it comes to unkind or hateful words. Words can have enormous potential for good or evil.

Sixth, sometimes God's Spirit may "call" us to go and get involved in a difficult situation. We may be the first responder and time is of the essence. We may need to "sniff out" the problem and apply ourselves to reach the objective.

Seventh, I think of the "air-drops" of nourishment and supplies to achieve what God calls us to do. He is faithful and will protect us and strengthen us to accomplish his will.

Are you ready for God's call to service? Have you equipped yourself with the "map" of his Word and the "tools" of love, joy, peace, patience, and other necessities? Are you in good spiritual health?

Finally, I remember the duff we had to deal with at the Dingford Creek fire. It was deep, dry, and dirty, and it stood in the way of getting the job done. Duff can accumulate in our lives as well. Over the years, we can let unconfessed sin, debilitating habits, and other debris build up and cover our once fertile hearts.

Fire can be destructive in a good sense in that it can clear our lives of impurities and make us whole inside. There are hymns and gospel songs that speak of the "fire from above."

When the Holy Spirit came upon the disciples in the Upper Room it appeared as "tongues of fire" over each person sitting there. Perhaps this needs to happen more often among the people called "Christians."

Do you need God to burn away the duff in your heart and cleanse you from stains of sin and impulses of self-will? He will do this as you surrender your life to him as fuel for his Holy Fire.

My heart an altar,
Thy love the flame.

Chapter 15

Surprised By Fire

After the forest fire blazed through our mountain property in 2001, I had a small logging outfit come in and remove more than a hundred damaged trees that were still standing. In one area, I asked one of the men to bulldoze out the stumps and pile them for burning.

A few years later I struck a match and set the pile on fire. For two days the fire ate away the stumps, finally bringing the pile nearly to ground level. On the third day before driving back to our apartment 110 miles away in Edmonds, Washington, I checked the remaining ashes and found no smoke or other sign of heat. The fire was dead.

The next weekend I cut down a green fir tree near the back porch so we could begin construction on a small addition. I trimmed the limbs off the tree and hauled them to where I had burned the stumps the weekend before. I unloaded the limbs on the ash heap and thought, "I'll burn this pile in the fall when the limbs are dry."

Two weekends later I cut down a dead tree and loaded some of the limbs and trunk pieces into a trailer. I took the load to the slash pile I mentioned above. Imagine my surprise to find that the green boughs I had unloaded two weeks before were gone! Only a few unburned pieces lay around the edge of the ash heap.

The fire I considered dead had been smoldering under the surface of the ground. When fuel was added, the sleeping fire rose through the ashes and consumed the green wood. I don't know when during those two weeks this happened, but somewhere along the line, the hidden heat burst into flames and consumed the fuel.

I had a similar experience during December of that year. When we arrived from Edmonds for the weekend, we found eight inches of snow on the ground and rainy weather. The wet stuff continued all day Saturday. The temperature was just above freezing so the rain soaked into the snow without melting it. Yet, in spite of the heavy rain, it was beautiful to see the land covered with a blanket of white.

Sunday morning I awoke around 3a.m. and saw a flickering light reflected on the window. I got up, looked outside, and saw what appeared to be a small fire in the middle of the snow about 120 yards from the house. Fire in snow?

I dressed, put on my boots, got a shovel and flashlight and tromped through the snow to the fire. There was a stump down in a hole burning vigorously.

Three weeks earlier I had burned a pile of slash around the stump, fully expecting that it would burn itself out after a few days. The absence of smoke and the presence of wet weather assisted my confidence. The presence of snow sealed the deal. This fire was out!

Yet, all the while it was "out," under the surface it smoldered until, even with a covering of snow and drenching rain, it suddenly surfaced.

It is true with us as well. We can deal with sin on the surface and never get down to the root of the problem where the hidden heat of evil resides. We may think we have our lives under control and may even appear cool and collected on the outside; but underneath, the heat of lust, greed, or other passions may smolder.

The desires of our flesh can be like hidden coals waiting to break loose when temptations come. We may think we are free of fire, but let the right circumstances arise and we are surprised to find otherwise.

There is only one sure way to put a fire out for good and that is by dousing the ashes with water—thoroughly, completely, totally inundating the area. This includes digging down into the ashes, stirring the ashes, and making sure every single ember is soaked. Forest rangers talk about using the "hand test" before leaving a campfire site. Don't be fooled by the absence of smoke.

Jesus said that our belief in him results in "streams of living water" bubbling up within us. He said this of his Spirit who works in our hearts to satisfy our deepest thirst and to deliver us from the fires of former cravings.

We can try to stomp out our passions and proceed with a self-controlled demeanor, assuming the fire is out. Or we can dig down deep and soak our souls with the cool, clear, loving Presence of God. He is willing and able to cleanse our hearts from the glowing coals of evil desire.

When you least expect it, a flame of lust or greed or anger may suddenly appear. When this happens, wield the shovel of repentance and dig down to the source. Swing the ax of faith to cut out the smoldering root. And then apply the cleansing, soothing Waters of God's Spirit to flood the depths of passion and vice.

Chapter 16

Rattlers Near Home ౿

The Western Rattlesnake is the only poisonous viper in Washington State. It is found mostly on the eastside of the Cascades where the climate is warmer and dryer. The skin of the snake is gray brown with large dark diamonds and narrow whitish lines. The head is brown and flat and the hollow fangs are retractable. It can open its mouth completely and slam needle-like fangs into prey where it releases its venom.

Though not normally aggressive, it can be provoked. I am told the bites sting and may cause severe illness; but they are rarely fatal. I prefer not to find out for myself.

Western Rattlesnakes can grow four-feet long, though local yore has one monster snake running close to seven feet. I used to think you could determine their age by the number of rattles, but apparently this is incorrect. However, there does seem to be a correlation between size and number of rattles. I also thought that these snakes could spring out of their coil a considerable distance. That notion is also wrong.

Oh, and I've been told that you cannot out-jerk a rattler. That is, if your hand is near a snake and you think you can withdraw it faster than the snake can strike, don't try it. The speed of the strike is like lightning.

During the six years we drove over the Cascades to spend weekends at our place in the Icicle Canyon, we encountered no snakes. I began to wonder about the stories I had heard. Then we moved to the canyon fulltime and the first summer we discovered three rattlers on our property.

The first sighting occurred when a young couple came to spend a weekend with us. They went out for a Saturday stroll and nearly stepped on a coiled rattler. Fortunately, it was in the cool of the morning and the young snake was just trying to keep warm and was a bit lethargic. While not attacked, our guests suffered emotional trauma.

The next weekend, Sandy was walking around the side of our home when she spied a coiled rattler apparently waiting for a chipmunk to walk by. Not wanting a poisonous creature so close to the house, I donned my eradication gear and ushered the snake to extinction.

Then, a day later, while I was working near the back porch, Sandy came over and reported a "large rattlesnake" by the woodpile. If the first snake was a youngster (three rattles) and the second, an older teen (six rattles) this one was a full blown adult with nine rattles. And it was fat.

When I arrived with my flat-edged shovel, he was stretched out a good 3.5 feet. I circled slowly to get in front of him and he lifted his head and followed my movement carefully. I stepped closer with the front of the shovel acting as a mini shield. Just then he started to "run" for the woodpile.

I lurched forward to nail him to the ground just behind his head.

My plan was to hold him there until Sandy could retrieve the pointed shovel with which I could swiftly remove his poisonous head. However, as I struck at the snake with the first shovel I caught only the edge of his body and had to lean the shovel downward at an angle to keep him pinned to the ground. By the time Sandy arrived with the other shovel, the angry snake had nearly broken loose.

Trying to keep him in place while I stabbed at him with the second shovel, I lessened the pressure on the first shovel and the viper wiggled free. Instead of heading for the woodpile, he came directly at me! He was hissing and rattling and his eyes blazed with vengeance. He was mad, mean, and malicious. When he was a mere foot away, I struck again and my sharp shovel found its mark.

After that close encounter, I have a new respect for these slithering creatures. In particular, I was able to later study the fangs and note their needle-sharp structure. These weapons are tough and long and can penetrate a leather boot.

Since that summer we have seen several more snakes near our mountain home. All met their maker. One day I went out the backdoor onto the deck. I was in the process of stepping off the deck to a flat rock 7 or 8 inches down when I saw the snake lying before me in the sun. Had I followed through with the step, my foot would have landed on the snake.

Another time I was descending the stairs from the kitchen and found a snake coiled at the base of the stairway. Again, had I not been vigilant, I would likely have suffered a snake bite.

When I encounter a rattler on the hillside or at a suitable distance from the house, I pause and let it move out of my way. I'm not out to eradicate rattlesnakes. I am, however, mighty watchful when I hike. I've also learned that these snakes are interested in self-preservation and will not challenge me without cause. And, of course, they do have a purpose in the grand scheme of things.

Still, I cannot tolerate a poisonous viper residing near my house. At times we have small children here, including our grandchildren. I don't want them innocently reaching down to pet a coiled rattler.

I know snakes are not evil and that they have their place. I also know the Bible likens Satan to a serpent, as well as a lion, and that these creatures have characteristics that provide insight into the enemy of our souls.

We are no match for that age-old serpent, the devil. Our little shovels will fail us every time. What we need is the shield of faith and the sword of truth. We need the Lord to walk before us as we walk the narrow Way.

I'm learning that you never know where or when a rattler may appear...and such is true of the devil. He may attack us through the poisonous lips of godless persons or tempt us in the chambers of our minds. Sometimes we can hear him hiss and rattle and other times he may seem lethargic and harmless. Always, we need to beware of his presence and to walk carefully in the steps of Jesus.

Chapter 17

An "Alarming" Story ↵

Since our home is 8 miles from town and off the utility grid, we take extra care to live safely and to be alert for fires and other dangers. This includes an ample supply of smoke and CO_2 detectors. Once a year we make the rounds and change batteries to keep the alarms in good working order. We are not only concerned with ourselves, but with those who visit us from time to time.

Living off the grid means we must create our own electricity and provide other utilities on site, such as water, heat, and sewage. We have a generator and six tanks ranging from 300 to 1,400 gallons for gas, diesel, propane, and water. Occasionally we have an outage or other emergency that requires immediate attention. I have learned a great deal about these things since we purchased the place in 1999.

Because of the wilderness location of the property and the potential for emergency repairs, we have been reluctant to invite guests to use the facilities when we are away. There are just too many things that can go wrong.

Several years ago we revisited our hesitations and decided to invite our former pastor and his wife to spend a week at "Alpenglow" during our absence. The power plant was running well and the other utilities seemed in good order. It was as good a time as any to follow our hospitality instincts and turn the keys over to someone who would enjoy the setting.

We heard that the pastor was on sabbatical leave but that he was as busy as ever. We planned to be gone, so they would have the entire place to themselves. The weather looked good and they were glad to get out of Seattle for several days.

They arrived the day we were leaving, so I had a chance to go over the basics with them. I made sure they had our cell phone numbers and other emergency numbers. They planned to spend five days, leaving the day of our return.

Everything was in order as we drove down the driveway. We felt good about having our friends enjoy the facilities and wonderful scenery.

The next morning I received a phone call from Pastor Mark. The carbon monoxide alarm was beeping downstairs where they were sleeping. "Must be the battery," I said. "I try to keep fresh batteries installed but maybe I overlooked this alarm. When they get low, they beep occasionally and I'm guessing that's the problem." So I told him where a replacement battery was and stayed on the phone with him until it was fixed. No more beeping so I wished them a pleasant day.

Another call. The alarm was sounding again. "It's an odd thing," he said. "When we open the door and windows, the alarm stops, but then when we shut things up again it starts beeping."

An "Alarming" Story

We ran some tests over the phone to see if the pilot lights were working on the downstairs water heater, fireplace, and refrigerator. Everything seemed to be in order.

I assured him there must be a problem with the alarm; perhaps he had not reset it correctly.

I called him later and learned he had removed the battery from the alarm to stop the beeping and that they were keeping the window open. "Good idea," I said. "I'll take care of things when I return."

When we arrived at the appointed time, I checked out the alarm and found it to be working correctly. Then I started to investigate the appliances and discovered that the burner on the propane fridge was sooty and not combusting fully. It needed a good cleaning.

I fixed the fridge and silenced the beeping.

I called the pastor to tell him what we had found and to profusely apologize for the problem they endured. I also expressed my profound relief that the two of them were still alive!

How do we respond to the beeping sounds of conscience? Do we disregard the warning? Do we downplay the danger? Do we disengage the annoying noise?

Since the "alarming" incident with our pastor and his wife, we have been far more responsive to beeping sounds, no matter when and where they sound. For example, a few weeks ago Sandy was awakened with what she thought were beeps emanating from the main floor of our house. We both went down to the kitchen to investigate.

We opened the door and windows and I went to work immediately on the propane fridge to clean the soiled burner.

As before with the basement fridge, we fixed the problem and reset the alarm. We're not taking any chances!

The Word of God reminds us that we live in hostile territory. The prince of the power of the air fills the atmosphere with poisonous fumes of partial truth.

By our own carelessness, we can jeopardize the spiritual health of others who inhabit our homes and the "dwellings" of friendship.

When the alarm of warning sounds, we must stop, track down the problem, and clean the burner of faith so the air we take into our spiritual lungs is fresh and pure.

Alarms are meant to alarm!

Chapter 18

Saga of the Red Truck

In November 2003 I purchased a new Ford 250 red pickup truck. It had heated leather seats, four-wheel-drive transmission, and hefty springs. I switched to larger and tougher tires and exchanged the running boards for chrome nerf bars. Every guy—at least around Leavenworth, Washington—had to have a pickup truck and I felt like "one of the boys" driving around in my red 250.

For seven years I used the 250 to haul wood, gravel, and personal cargo. I employed it to help people move their belongings and to drive the mountain passes in the snow. By January 2010 the odometer read 77,000 miles and I had every intention of keeping the vehicle for another seven years.

In early 2010 Sandy and I drove the truck to a motel near a senior community in Stanwood, Washington where my dad lived. We checked out in the morning and walked to the parking lot to unlock the truck and drive away.

A car sat in the parking space we had claimed the night before. The truck was gone—stolen in the night.

After calling the police and filling out a report, we arranged for transportation. The officer invited me to view the surveillance camera tape with him. The dastardly deed was filmed in progress.

Shortly after we arrived, a pickup truck similar to ours rolled into the lot and parked next to us. A man got out on the passenger side and seemed to fiddle with the door lock. Then he re-entered his truck and they drove to another parking place nearby. For one hour the two thieves sat in their truck waiting.

Apparently convinced we were in our room to stay, the man got out of the passenger side again and strolled over to our truck. We could tell he was short and stocky, but his head and face were hidden behind a drooping hat. It was too dark to determine other features or their license plate.

He opened the door and within a few seconds started the truck and pulled out of the lot with the other truck following. My treasured red pickup disappeared into the night, possibly heading to a chop shop to be disassembled for parts.

It took six weeks and lots of paperwork for the insurance company to pay me for the stolen truck. We thought about getting another truck, but decided to wait and get by with what we had.

Three months later the phone rang and the police in Bothell, Washington reported the recovery of my truck. Well, by then it wasn't my truck anymore; it belonged to the insurance company and they would determine its destiny.

Through a series of phone calls over the next few days, I learned that the truck was taken to an auto auction place for dealers in south Seattle where damaged or stolen vehicles were sold to the highest bidder. I gained permission to attend the auction even though I wasn't a dealer.

The morning of the sale, we left home early to arrive in Seattle at 8 a.m. in time to fill out the paperwork to participate in the auction. Nearly 700 vehicles were on tap for the day, about average for the weekly event. We sat in the bleachers and watched the proceedings as each car was driven to the front and the bidding commenced. Our truck was near the end of the list so we had plenty of time to learn the ropes and try to ascertain the wording of the rapid-speaking auctioneer.

Finally "our" truck neared the stage and I walked down to the railing to get close to the action. The auctioneer's assistant, who had been moving around in front of the crowd keeping things going, saw me and came over. He had noticed us in the stands all day. "Well, are you ready now?" he asked.

"Yeah, I'm after that red truck over there. It used to be mine and was stolen. I want to bid on it but I don't understand 90 percent of what the auctioneer is saying." He said he'd stick with me and help me. Then he went over to the auctioneer and told him what I had said.

The bidding started low and moved up rapidly. Seems like everyone wanted "my" truck. Finally only two of us were bidding and the other guy dropped out just before I reached my predetermined limit.

I should say that the truck, though filthy, seemed no less the worse for what it had been through. The body was in good shape and all systems seemed to work okay—except for the door and ignition locks.

We paid the price and drove back to Leavenworth in a two-vehicle celebratory parade—Sandy in her station wagon and me in my truck. The lost had been found, the stolen vehicle redeemed. What I had owned before was now mine again.

We had the repairs made and the truck detailed. It was cleaned and polished inside and out. Better than ever!

I'm sure you have already made the theological connections. We who once belonged to God fell into the hands of the serpent-thief where, like the rest of humankind, we lived without God and without hope. But thanks be to God, Jesus came to rescue us and outbid every contender by giving his life to redeem our souls.

Now we belong to him not only as his creation but also as his purchased children. We are twice-his and we live as crimson-washed vehicles of his grace and working vessels of his mercy. We transport his love to others and deliver kindnesses in his name.

To press the analogy further, we are fueled by his Holy Spirit and we roll down the highway of holiness, honking now and then just because we love Jesus. We swerve from temptation and brake to negotiate rough stretches of road. Music fills the cab of our hearts as we travel toward the eternal Land of Promise.

And when we park for the night, we sleep in peace for we have a vigilant watchman who keeps us in his care.

Chapter 19

Auto Mishaps

I had a fender bender at age 15, before I had a driver's license. A student at Seattle Pacific College permitted me to drive his car around Queen Anne Hill in Seattle. Another "youngster" hit me from behind with his dad's car. He had just turned 16. Fortunately, parents on both sides worked things out and we were able to avoid police and insurance involvement. The college student was amazingly understanding and forgiving.

My next auto mishap took place two years later when I was a passenger in a friend's car. It was, I think, a 1941 Dodge. We were on the south side of Queen Anne Hill, nearly to the waters of Elliott Bay.

We sat at a stop sign waiting for the traffic to clear. We had to cross two lanes of a busy road at rush hour and turn left into the inside lane going east. As we cleared the first two lanes and turned left, a large delivery truck struck us at the right front corner, spinning us around and into the two lanes we had just passed. A blue 1955 Oldsmobile going west hit us and spun us again and into the side of a passing Metro Bus.

We were both thrown from the car. I smashed the passenger door with my shoulder and head and slid out and onto the wet pavement, skidding across the pavement on my back toward the oncoming traffic. I vividly recall seeing the cars in both northbound lanes sliding to a stop as they tried to avoid the accident. When the sliding stopped, my head was directly under the bumper of a car. I remember reaching up and pulling myself to my feet and going to check on my friend who was lying on the pavement. He had followed me out of the car on his back and was unhurt. The wet surface probably helped us from losing skin.

Everything was at a standstill. His car was a mangled mess with bits and pieces littering three lanes. People just stared in disbelief. An older woman who had been walking on the sidewalk came over to me in tears to ask if I was alright and to say how lucky I was to be alive.

There was a gas station right there on the corner and I walked over to call the police. I actually had to borrow a dime from the attendant to use the pay phone to make the call. At the time, and more so now, I recall how paralyzed everyone seemed to be.

I'm foggy on what happened next. I think we were checked out by emergency people and pronounced okay. I know we didn't go to the hospital. The remains of my friend's car were taken to a wrecking yard and someone came and drove us home. The only aftereffect I recall was a sore shoulder and bits of glass inside my pants. Surely the Lord had his hand on two teenagers that day.

While I think my friend was a good driver for his age, the crowded roads and rainy weather made it difficult to watch all potential hazards and make a quick and safe decision. That truck seemed to come out of nowhere.

This is so true about temptation. Sometimes it materializes when we least expect it, or when we are tired or distracted. Sometimes it comes gently and subtly, while at other times it hits us like a truck—a delivery truck with unwanted cargo.

Someone has said, "Life is fragile, handle with prayer." This means carefully watching for "enemy traffic" that bears down upon us with evil intent. It means using brakes or acceleration when required. The Lord's Prayer teaches us to pray, "Lead us not into temptation." In other words, the best way to be safe is to avoid temptation. In the rush of life, keep alert, watch and pray.

Another auto mishap: This one occurred when I was pastoring a church in North Seattle. My wife and two-year-old daughter were in the car with me as we travelled along residential streets to the home of a parishioner. Sandy had the child on her lap as she tried to comb her hair in preparation for the visit.

As we entered an intersection, a car suddenly appeared to the right and slammed into the side of our vehicle, spraying broken glass everywhere, especially in the back seat where our daughter normally would have been sitting.

No one was hurt, but a direct hit on the passenger door could have been crippling or worse. The driver of the other car failed to observe a "Yield" sign and readily admitted that the accident was his fault. Interestingly, I knew the man through my associations with Seattle Pacific University.

Whether a delivery truck on busy Elliott Avenue or a passenger car on a quiet residential street, we must live in perpetual watchfulness.

The fourth auto mishap occurred while speeding westward from Detroit on I-94. It was past midnight and I was a passenger in my own car. I was so tired that I couldn't stay awake, so I switched places with my passenger...and then fell fast asleep. Unfortunately, the driver also succumbed to sleep.

The next thing I knew we were sliding sideways on the grass median that separated the two directions of traffic. We didn't spin around or roll over or hit anything; we just slid along until we came to a stop.

How absolutely terrifying to wake to that kind of danger! We could have been killed so easily, or seriously injured. Instead, we simply slid sideways.

After sitting there a few moments to gather our wits, we drove back onto the freeway and continued on our way. Since then I've been unable to sleep in a moving car.

Sliding sideways happens when we fall asleep at the wheel spiritually. We enter a danger zone where we are vulnerable to accident and harm. We lose focus and traction and finally come to a stop. Sitting sideways in the middle between two directions, we are like the lukewarm folks at the Laodicean church described in the Book of Revelation.

When we finally wake up and recognize our hazardous plight, we best confess our failure and get right back on the road to our desired destination.

The incident on I-94 also causes me to reflect on Psalm 121 where we are told that God, our watchful Father, never slumbers nor sleeps. He is always on the job, always loving us with observant care.

My horrific freeway experience is a powerful reminder that we can only trust our family and friends so far. In spite of their best intentions, they will inevitably let us down.

Consider the inner circle of disciples who disappointed Jesus as he prayed in the garden. They were to stand watch, yet three times they fell asleep. The spirit was willing, but the flesh was weak.

I'm so thankful we can trust the steering wheel of our lives to the One who knows the road and who is ever watchful. We can rest safely in him for he will never fail us nor forsake us.

Chapter 20

Skunk in the Parsonage ❧

A few years after we were married, Sandy and I moved to Ellensburg, Washington to pastor a small Free Methodist Church. The people were very good to us and we enjoyed our time there.

One Sunday afternoon, a couple took us for a scenic ride in their new car. As we came off the freeway and rounded the off-ramp, we saw a tiny skunk at the side of the road. How it got there we could not tell, but we stopped and saw that it had been born only recently. No mama skunk was in sight.

"Let's take it home," I said. "We can nurse it and maybe keep it as a pet."

So the driver opened the trunk and we set the little creature on a rag.

Back at the parsonage, we carefully fed the little skunk and she began to grow. We called her Daisy.

When I told a veterinarian friend of mine about the skunk, he advised me to have Daisy de-scented. "I'll do it for nothing," he said. "Just bring her to the office tomorrow morning. It won't take long."

The next day I was there first thing in the morning with our new pet. He said, "Let's go outside in the back, just in case something smelly happens."

He took a glass canning jar and put some ether-soaked cotton inside. He placed the skunk in the jar headfirst. He then showed me the two "perfume" sacks and said, "All I have to do is cut these sacks out and she'll be harmless."

As he picked up his scalpel, he commented he needed to be very careful not to nick the sack because fluid would shoot out and stink up the neighborhood. Small skunks are extra potent. He said, "I usually work with my hands under a plate of glass to protect my face, but I think we'll be okay today doing it this way."

With that, he went to work carefully cutting around one of the sacks to remove it. Ooops. He cut the sack and fluid sprayed his face and shirt. I was out of the line of fire.

Muttering words unfit for my pastoral ears, he finished removing the sack and started on the second one. Same thing happened.

I retrieved the skunk from the jar and put her in a little box. The vet peeled off his shirt and turned on a garden hose to wash his face, hair, and arms. The invectives continued, though somewhat more controlled. I fought mightily to keep from laughing.

To say the vet and the surrounding area reeked of skunk smell would not adequately capture the moment as he walked to the back door of his office. He opened the door and yelled to his assistant, "I've got to go home and take a bath. I won't be in for the rest of the day!"

I thanked him for his help, expressed my condolences, and drove Daisy away from the offensive odor.

Skunk in the Parsonage

We kept the skunk for several months. She lived with us in the parsonage and we all got along fairly well. With her defenses gone, she was vulnerable to wandering canines in the neighborhood.

Skunks are nocturnal, so generally they sleep during the day and become active at night. She liked to hide under the couch and when we went to bed, we'd hear her making little sounds around the house.

We didn't tell visitors about the skunk in the house because we didn't want to alarm them. Chances are, the people would come and go and never know. But not always.

Once we had a rather rotund woman visiting us, a relative from Michigan. She was sitting in a chair when Daisy made her appearance from under the couch. When the woman saw the skunk, she pierced the air of our quiet little town with her screams. At the same time, she made herself into a large ball on the chair and squealed uncontrollably until we got Daisy out of the room.

Another time we had a woman and her young daughter visiting us. The two guests were just coming out of a bedroom when they saw Daisy ducking into one of the rooms in the hallway. The mother grabbed her daughter and nearly knocked Sandy over as she ran down the hall and out the front door screaming, "There's a skunk in the house! There's a skunk in the house!"

We had a litter box for Daisy to use, and at first it worked well. Then, for some unexplained reason, she began to favor my shoes. This did not please me.

A few months after acquiring Daisy, we came home from the evening service and found an empty house. We searched high and low for the skunk, but with no luck. We finally concluded that she had managed to get into the dryer air vet and then on to the outside world.

We concluded that, lacking her defensive mechanism, our little pet likely met with foul play.

Okay, what are the personal applications we can draw from Daisy? Can we glean anything worthwhile?

First, skunks belong in the out-of-doors. I know that some would disagree with me, but my experience suggests otherwise. We had fun with her, but she never reached the status of "man's best friend." Skunks belong in the wilds, not in the living room.

Likewise, there are some things that simply do not belong in the living rooms of our hearts. You can't turn an evil habit into a nice pet. Better to keep the door shut against practices that can scare people and make messes in unwanted places.

Second, some might say that there is something particularly inappropriate about a pastor having a skunk for a pet. Some of my parishioners seemed to lack enthusiasm. I don't know exactly why, but they found the two images incongruent. They couldn't quite get their minds around the idea of a skunk living in the parsonage.

The Bible teaches us to avoid the very appearance of evil. This would certainly apply to keeping undesirable ideas in the dark places of our minds. We are to select associations that are compatible with the sweet aroma of the Gospel.

Third, our Daisy was defenseless. When danger, like a dog, would come near she would stomp her front feet and twist her backside around to blast the enemy. Trouble was, she didn't have any ammo.

Just so, we can become defenseless spiritually when we fail to maintain the weapons of faith and the Word of God. We need to sustain a good stockpile of ordinance to wage war against the adversary of our souls.

A final word: I realize there are people who adore skunks, keep them as pets, and participate in festivals celebrating them. You can see all of this on YouTube. However, we've chosen to leave skunks alone and let them live free.

Are you wondering about the veterinarian? He said it took him three days to get rid of the smell.

Chapter 21

The Yucky Tongue ℰↄ

As a young pastor in Ellensburg, Washington—back in the late '60s—I incorporated a "children's sermon" into the Sunday morning services. I had the kids come up to the front and sit on the floor. Then I'd sit down with them and tell a story or show an object lesson and apply the truth to their young hearts.

Occasionally I'd glance up and see the teens and adults in the congregation leaning forward. They liked this part of the morning as well. Sometimes, after the service, an adult might shake my hand at the door and thank me for the children's talk. My 30-minute sermon went in one ear and out the other, but the object lesson with the kids hit home.

Sometimes I worked on the children's sermon as much as my main message. I was always trying to come up with something fresh and interesting, something that would make an indelible impression. At times I was able to tie both sermons together.

One week I started to think about the tongue. I looked up various verses in the Bible that warn of the horrible consequences of an ungodly tongue, and of the blessings a "good" tongue could bestow. But how could I demonstrate this? What could I show to make a lasting impression?

There's a verse that compares the tongue with a flame of fire that can set a whole forest ablaze. But burning down the building to make a point didn't seem appropriate. Then there's the passage that speaks of bridling the tongue. I toyed with the idea of bringing a horse inside to show how a bridle works. But again, I opted for discretion.

Then a flash of true inspiration burst in my brain: I will go to the meat market and get a cow tongue and pass it around!

So I did. I got the biggest, ugliest tongue I could find and put it in a large zip-lock bag. I squeezed out the air so you could feel the shape and softness of the tongue. I stored it in the fridge.

Sunday came and I called the children forward. Then I retrieved the tongue from behind the pulpit and asked them what it was. I think one little farm boy got it right away. I explained that it was a cow's tongue and that no one in the congregation had made a sacrificial offering for the children's sermon.

After the kids looked it over, I passed it around the congregation. Eeuuu! Gross! Augggggghhhhh!

Then, amid the discomfort, I challenged everyone—young and old—to guard their own tongues and to use them only for speaking words of kindness, encouragement, and blessing.

Of all the object lessons I gave at that church, this one passed the test of time. I say that because even today when I bump into a former parishioner I sometimes hear about that Sunday morning.

Later, in another church, I gave a children's sermon almost every Sunday for four years. I've forgotten most of them, but not the one about the can of beans. Before the service, I took a can of beans and carefully removed the wraparound label. I replaced it with a label from a can of corn. Then, with children seated around me, I held up the can and asked them what was inside.

They could see the label clearly and said in unison, "Corn." I asked them how they knew that and they pointed to the label. I said, "Well, maybe it's something different. Maybe there are peaches or carrots in there."

They were adamant: "It's corn! Can't you see the label?"

I said, "There's only one way to find out. Does anyone have a can opener?"

When no one could come up with an opener, I produced one and proceeded to open the can. The kids were hanging over me, watching intently. Then I poured the contents into a clear glass bowl—beans!

I went on to make the point that it's what is inside of us that counts. We can wear smiley faces and everyone will think we are happy. Yet inside we may be sad. And sometimes we may appear nice to others, while inside we are not so nice. I'm not so sure about the children, but the adults got the point.

Another Sunday I passed around a flashlight to the kids and asked them to turn it on. It didn't work and I asked them why. A smart kid in the front said, "The batteries are dead."

So I unscrewed the bottom of the flashlight and removed the batteries. Then I put new batteries inside and handed it to the kid. Still no light.

"There must be another problem. What is it?" I asked. Then I unscrewed the top where the bulb is located. "Hey! Look here! Something is blocking the power from reaching the bulb."

I proceeded to pull out a small, thin piece of cloth with a word inscribed by a felt-tip pen, "Lying." I then pulled out another piece. This one read, "Stealing." Another read, "Bad

Words." Then I proceeded to make the application that the light of Jesus cannot shine through our lives when we do bad things.

Over the years I've lost track of the kids who gathered around me on Sunday mornings. I wonder if they remember the sermonettes and if my efforts had any lasting effect.

One thing I do know is that some of those sermons have stayed with me over the years. The truth they sought to convey is still valid today.

Our tongues can cause either pain or happiness. We can wear false labels that make us hypocritical in God's eyes. And we can allow thoughts and behaviors to block the sunshine of God's love flowing through our lives.

Chapter 22

Spring Break ℰ↷

According to the dictionary, the term "spring break" is "a vacation from school or college during the spring term, lasting about a week." I really didn't need the dictionary to tell me that because, like you, I discovered the meaning on my own. Every year from high school through seminary I joined millions of other students in an assortment of recreational activities to blow off steam and prepare for the last grueling round of classes before the summer months.

I am trying to recount the spring breaks I experienced during my educational career since entering high school. Three observations come to light. First, I can't remember every spring break of my past. Some are simply lost to antiquity. They must have been pretty dull.

Second, of the ones I recall, I find a variety of activities, ranging from a few concert choir tours, a mission trip, and vacations of one sort or another.

Third, it seems the breaks I recall best are those etched on my mind because of at least one unusual occurrence. A couple of breaks claim more than a few memorable happenings.

For example, when I was a senior in high school, a friend and I decided to escape Seattle and head for some unknown location—just for the fun of it. We located a map of the Western United States and laid it out on a table. Then we put the index fingers of our right hands together, closed our eyes, and turned around awkwardly two or three times. In our disoriented state, we found the table and directed our fingers to land on the map.

When we opened our eyes, we found our fingers pointing to Winnemucca, Nevada. We had never heard of the place and yet in that moment it became our spring break destination.

For two weeks we planned and acquired all the things we thought we would need, including grubby clothes and camping gear. Mostly, we scrounged around for cash. We pooled all of the money we could acquire and put it into a tin can. Since he had the more reliable car, he volunteered to drive.

A day or two before our departure, we raided the cupboards of both kitchens. The more grub we could take, the less money we'd have to spend. Our mothers, especially, were eager to send us off with an ample supply of food.

Someone took our photo the day of our departure, perhaps thinking we might never return.

I can recall several things about that trip with Deane. There were tense times of disagreement and happy times of laughing together in the middle of the night. Once, while Deane was driving, I fell fast asleep. I awoke with a start around midnight to find the car parked alongside the highway. I couldn't locate Deane right away and wondered what was going on. Then I looked out the window and found him sitting on the front fender viewing a drive-in theater screen from the shoulder of the highway. I went out and joined him on the other fender.

One night the car generator went out and we had to use battery power to limp into a small town. We found an auto shop on the main drag and parked in front, hoping for some sleep before the place opened. It was during that long sleepless night that we discovered an unopened box of prunes in one of the food boxes. By morning, the box was empty. You can take it from there.

When we finally made it to Winnemucca, we got out and tried to undo the sign at the edge of town. We wanted it for a souvenir. However, we soon abandoned our efforts, fearing detection and possible arrest. A healthy dose of guilt and the possibility of our parents learning of a theft and capture in Nevada settled the matter.

We drove into town and looked around. This triumphant tour of our destination location took about two minutes. Then we started for home. Winnemucca—at least at that time—was not a place to write home about.

One night, driving through a vast stretch of desert we ran out of steam. We were so tired we had to stop and sleep. We found what appeared to be a side road and pulled off the highway. Still unsure whether it was a road, we drove into the desert a short distance and shut off the motor. We conked out almost immediately.

Later, in the darkest hour, we awoke to a rumbling sound. We saw a bright light bearing down on us from out in the desert. It seemed to be paralleling the road. It grew closer and louder, filling us with terror. Suddenly we realized it was a train and it was heading straight for us. At least it appeared that way. Before we could start the car and drive away or get out and run to the highway, the locomotive and a mile of box cars roared by about 25 feet from where we sat shuttering in the car. We had no idea there were train tracks anywhere near us.

That did it for sleeping. Off again we went on our trip back to Seattle.

Someplace in Northern California, we decided to camp by a lake we had located on the map. We stopped at a little store and bought some hot dogs, buns, and marshmallows. We found the gravel road leading to the lake and started down. Periodically, we passed signs that read, "No Camp Fires Allowed." Since we were planning to cook our meal over an open fire, we looked the other way when we saw more signs ahead of us.

We found a vacant campground where the road met the lake. We kept going and drove around the lake where we found an undesignated camping spot. Here we could look across the water and monitor any cars coming down the road.

It was late afternoon as we prepared our little campsite. We laid out a tarp for our sleeping bags and fixed a fire circle. Then we gathered wood and cut roasting sticks for the wieners and marshmallows.

We waited until dusk to light the fire. Just as we were about to roast the hot dogs, we saw the lights of a vehicle coming down the road across the lake. Fearing we would be caught and flogged for disobeying the no-fire rule, we hurriedly kicked dirt on the fire to put it out.

The vehicle started to come around the end of the lake and we just knew it would be a ranger or policeman. With the fire out, but still smoking slightly, we drove the car over top of it to conceal our wrongdoing.

We steadied ourselves and readied our look of innocence. Two guys in their 20s got out of the vehicle and walked over. "What's happening?" one asked. Small talk followed. Then one of them pointed and said, "Hey, is that smoke coming out from under your car?"

We told them about our efforts to hide our fire and they guffawed. They were still laughing when they drove away to the other side of the lake. Fortunately, the fire didn't reignite while covered by the car. Now *that* would have been a story to write about.

Three years later, this time as a college junior, I joined four classmates on a spring break adventure that took us to Disneyland in Southern California. My roommate was from La Habra and assured us that his folks would welcome us for a few days of R&R. He also had a car and was planning to drive home anyway.

At the end of our last exam, we tossed our gear in the trunk and headed south. Four of us were six feet or taller and the fifth guy, though considerably shorter, outweighed any of us. We needed a shoehorn to get us all into the car.

Our plan was to drive straight through, stopping for our first meal in Portland, Oregon. I knew of a great place to eat and so we skipped lunch at the school cafeteria and set our sights on a hearty dinner in Portland. The special thing about this particular restaurant was the price: "All you can eat for 99 cents."

It was Friday night and people were pouring into the restaurant when we arrived. We located a table for five in the middle of a large open eating area. Having laid claim to the table, we headed for the buffet. Because of our collective experience in eating at such places, we wisely passed by the salads and headed for the entrées, heaping our plates with meat, potatoes, and other solids.

We returned to our table and began devouring our meals like famished lions. Then, one by one, we'd get up and visit the buffet tables for more. It was like we had bottomless stomachs. People at nearby tables began to comment about our appetites.

Next came the dessert buffet and again we set out to break every eating record known to man. More people in the crowded restaurant pointed and smiled. I'm not sure of this, but it is possible some of them were making wagers to see which one of us would claim the prize.

It was during the time we were gorging ourselves with desserts that the silliness of it all struck us. We began to chuckle about the spectacle we were making and soon we were laughing aloud. I actually laughed so hard I fell over backward in my chair. We couldn't stop laughing! Eventually, the manager made his way over to us and politely requested that we leave.

If it took a shoehorn to get us into the car earlier, this time required unbelievable contortions and a combination of pushes and pulls. But we made it, and down the highway we sped toward the warm sun of the South.

We were so full and it was so cramped in the car that we moaned and groaned most of the way. By the time we arrived we were stiff, sore, and cranky. I think we slept for two days before going to Disneyland.

We had a great time at the theme park seeing the sights and riding the rides. That night we were telling our hosts about our adventures when they asked, "Did you ride the _____? That's the best ride in the park!" We looked at each other blankly. No one remembered even seeing that ride. Elation turned to disappointment as we realized we had driven a thousand miles to visit Disneyland and missed the best ride of all.

I have tried to recall whether or not we stopped by the 99-cent place on our return trip. I'm guessing we skipped it for fear the manager would remember us. In any case, we made it home in one piece, achy and tired, but still friends; and still wondering what it would have been like to go on "the greatest ride at Disneyland."

What possible lessons can we learn from these two spring breaks? The campfire incident on the Winnemucca trip might serve to remind us of the futility of trying to hide our sins. When we attempt to cover up wrongdoing, the truth seeps out one way or another. Better to live openly and honestly before God and others.

The trip to Disneyland cautions us about the negative example we set by gluttonous behavior and out-of-control humor. The witness of our lives will linger more as a joke than a redemptive example when we act the fool. Self-control is a virtue worth fostering, even in the midst of hilarity.

We are designed for spring breaks. Not just the high school and college variety, but for anytime during the year when we need to step aside and quiet ourselves and perhaps have a wholesome laugh. The whole idea of the Sabbath is built about our need for periodic rest. The problem we have is using our down times to busy ourselves with all manner of activity. We jam our breaks so full that it takes us a week to recuperate afterward.

Jesus invited his disciples to come with him to a quiet place for some much needed rest. This invitation to take a break from the busyness of life is still valid today. It may or may not involve Disneyland or even a trip to Winnemucca. It will, however, include rest of body and mind, and happy communion with Jesus our Savior and Friend.

Chapter 23

Living in Joy Hall ℰᵔ

After graduating from seminary in 1964 and getting married that summer, I took my bride to Greenville College in Central Illinois where we lived and worked for two years. I taught Bible courses, administered the campus chapel program and, together with my student-wife, served as house parents for one year in the upper-class men's dormitory, Joy Hall.

We lived in a small fish-bowl apartment just off the first floor lobby. Outside our door, the TV blared constantly and boisterous students passed by to go in and out the main door. The floors were polished linoleum and the walls, plaster. The whole place—lobby, halls, and especially our apartment—was an echo chamber that seemed to magnify every sound.

Other than a small bathroom, our apartment included two rooms: a living/dining/kitchen combination and a bedroom. The walls were thin and from our bedroom we could discern the conversations next door. Of course, the opposite was true as well.

We had a turquoise Naugahyde couch, two chairs, and a kitchen table. The bedroom boasted of one bed, one dresser, one chair, and a small closet. Our windows looked out on a small grassy area and onto the windows of an adjacent dorm. We kept the curtains closed.

Our Greenville stay happened during the era of segregated dorms and restricted hours. Since our inhabitants were upperclassmen, they had more liberties than the freshmen and sophomores. However, "our boys" still had to sign out when they left and sign back in upon return. I didn't tout my authority in this area and pretty much followed the honor system.

But not the Dean of Men. He was particularly vigilant regarding the rules and any infractions—especially if they included co-ed interactions past the "lock down" time. Once he was caught hiding in a tree to spy on suspected violators. News of that unfortunate event spread quickly through the campus and for the next week he became the butt of nearly every joke. Any moral authority the Dean might have had dissipated rapidly.

Other stories come to mind, including the time I stood to introduce the renowned chapel speaker who had come from St. Louis...and noticed a frog hopping down the center aisle. Or the time multiple alarm clocks went off while a nationally known speaker was waxing eloquent.

I also recall a few class lectures when I put both feet into my mouth. Oh yes, there are many tales related to our two-year stay at Greenville. But let me return to Joy Hall.

My office was a closet-sized room and the first door to the left off the lobby and down the first floor hall. No windows. Besides a small desk and two chairs, I had a bookcase overcrowded with college and seminary books, and others I had acquired along the way. It is a good thing I'm not claustrophobic because this office would have done me in.

In short, we lived in the thick of things and we were never really alone. We could not have marital spats because the noise would carry, news would spread, and we'd be the object of next-day grins. So our little tiffs had to be silent simmering things that waited fuller expression until we were well outside the dorm—usually in the car away from campus.

Once, when Sandy was vacuuming, she started to sing "Old Man River." Moments later, applause and laughter erupted from the dwellers in the next room. She sang no more.

One evening a knock came and when I opened the door I found a resident assistant trembling with rage. He blurted out: "Someone stole my door!" We found it hidden in an adjacent building.

Then there was the evening when practically every guy in the dorm was crammed into the second-floor hallway demanding that a student (with poor personal hygiene) take a shower. I told everyone to get inside a nearby room and let me handle it. As I stood at the guy's door trying to reason with him, I looked down the hall to see stacks of faces peering from the doorways. When the guy came out to head for the showers, he addressed his protagonists with terms unfit to repeat.

More than once I spent late night hours counseling students about their self-doubts and awkward feelings about girls. I recall finals week and noisy all-night study sessions and golf balls bouncing on the floor overhead.

Sometimes I wonder how we ever made it through our first year!

But we did make it and, as you can see, we have a few memories to smile about. If I think hard enough, I am also reminded of the good times. The popcorn and stories. The prayer times. Friendships. Victories. This all occurred in a place called Joy.

Our little dormitory domicile is not unlike the space each of us inhabits daily. We live, as it were, on display and our behavior and attitudes are noted by others. Our actions reverberate throughout the halls of our responsibilities and acquaintances.

We are interrupted time and again with the importune knocks of annoyance. Some people we enjoy; others we endure. Some days go well, others weary us. Leaky faucets, noisy hallways, snoopy people, missing doors, bull sessions, bouncing golf balls, tears, laughter—they all confront us in the campus housing we call life.

Through it all, as we prepare for Graduation, we are learning to become more like the Master. We are gathering wisdom and insight and growing in patience. We are finding that our residency on this earth is both challenging and rewarding.

Life is worth living in "Joy Hall."

Chapter 24

Odd Jobs

Never guess a woman's age. I learned that simple truth the summer I worked at a coffee company in downtown Seattle. This was well before Starbucks and other names you'd easily recognize. You would probably even know this company's name because it is still operating, not only in Seattle but now throughout the United States.

I don't recall what summer I worked there, nor do I remember the wages. What does stick in my mind are the people I worked with—an interesting and colorful combination of employees who had been with the company for many years. It was like family.

Green coffee beans were imported from distant lands and roasted daily right there in the building. You could smell the delightful aroma for blocks. Beans were blended and ground with exacting skill. The five pound bags were then rushed to area restaurants where fresh cups of coffee delighted customers. A café or restaurant that could boast of freshly roasted coffee was assured of a regular and enthusiastic clientele.

My job that summer was to fill in for people who were gone for a few weeks of vacation. This was great because I got to do lots of different things. For example, one time I was responsible for stacking newly arrived sacks of coffee beans, and for lugging the rightly identified beans to the roasting oven. It was hard work and I was glad when the muscle-bound employee returned.

One room was set aside with countertops holding small glass cups and other items. I learned that this was the tasting room where the blends were analyzed and corrected as necessary. I stuck my head in on several occasions and watched white-coated men and women sipping coffee and making mouth noises as they tried to reach consensus on the quality of taste.

After tasting part of one cup, they would rinse out their mouths and then try another cup. The process took quite a while, and I am sure they all left the room high on caffeine. Interestingly, not everyone was a "taste scientist." A few longtime employees were pretty good at it as well and were often called upon to join the professional testers.

I think everyone who worked at the company drank coffee—and only coffee produced right there in-house. During coffee breaks we'd gather in the break room and enjoy freshly roasted, ground, and brewed coffee. As I recall, these breaks usually extended beyond the allotted time.

After the coffee beans were blended and ground, they were poured into five-pound bags and placed on a conveyer belt. The labeled bags were then closed, sealed, and sent on to shipping. Here they were either set aside to fill small orders or packed into boxes for the larger restaurants. Trucks were loaded and the drivers fanned out across the city to deliver the coveted product.

For two weeks I worked at the end of the conveyer belt with a woman who was spry, talkative, and nosy. I seemed to get along well with her and found she could take kidding, as well as dish it out.

One day the subject of age came up. Acting cocky, I asked, "I bet I can guess your age." She was game so I began to calculate the years based on what I had learned about her. I knew she was married, had two kids, and had worked at the company 20 years.

I thought, okay, she probably got married around 21, raised her kids at least until grade school, worked at a couple of places for maybe six years, and then put in 20 years in her current job. I took into account her appearance—the wear and tear of the years. It seemed pretty obvious to me that she was at least 52.

When I confidently declared my conclusion, I knew instantly I had made a grievous error. She huffed and puffed and read me the riot act. Nearby employees looked at me sympathetically. For the rest of the summer I was unable to restore the amiable relationship we had shared earlier.

She was 39! She had married at 16, had kids right away and went to work at 19. Her first job was her current job. Add it all together and you have 39—13 years younger than my estimate.

I have never, ever tried to guess a woman's age since that summer.

A year or two later, I experienced another "odd" job at a company just a few blocks away from the coffee place. This company made footlockers. A friend of mine and I both applied for the two positions, thinking we could share rides and have some fun working together.

This was not a large business, but they did turn out a good variety and supply of metal trunks. The boss took us around and introduced us as the new "shipping team" and showed us how to ready the trunks for delivery. It seemed like "a piece of cake" and we were confident we could complete our daily assignment in good fashion.

I should mention that the other employees had been there for umpteen years and were all of vintage age. Also, they seemed to work in slow motion.

Nonetheless, my friend and I dove into our responsibilities with great zeal. Before noon we had all of the completed trunks wrapped and ready for shipping. The boss expressed pleasure and urged the other workers to pick up the pace so we would have more work to do.

While we stood around waiting for the next batch of trunks, the workers shot daggers at us and grumbled that we "young bucks" had upset the applecart. They groused among themselves and complained to the boss. By the second afternoon unprintable words reached our tender ears and we realized that our work ethic had disrupted the status quo.

We went to the boss and reported the problem as we saw it. We said, "We're thinking maybe we should go so things can get back to normal." He agreed and wrote us both a check for our time. It was the shortest job either of us ever experienced.

Over the years I've had many odd jobs. I remember delivering newspapers, mowing lawns, selling subscriptions, working on a farm, notifying gas customers of a coming change, delivering Christmas packages for the postal service, waiting tables, telephone operator at seminary, warehouse manager and delivery man, marina gopher, night watchman, summer camp director, music minister, youth pastor, and so forth.

One of the more interesting jobs was "guaranteed" to make me rich. It was a multi-level marketing scheme that revolved around water purification units. A friend introduced me to this "incredible opportunity" and I was ushered into a high pressure network of not only selling filters myself, but enlisting others who would work for me, even as I worked for the guy ahead of me. I bought a small supply of filters and marketing materials. I started to go to sales meetings. I made house calls on friends I thought might be interested.

Only one problem: nobody wanted the filters. And I had zero success enlisting my own team of sales people. The whole thing fizzled out within a month.

Over time I have managed to give or throw away the remnants of that depressing experience. I was sorry to disappoint my friend, but glad when I broke free from that money-grubbing endeavor.

We all have our own stories of jobs we liked or disliked. In fact, a good hunk of our lives is devoted to employment— whether for ourselves or for others. Work is part of life and through it we find both fulfillment and frustration.

Beyond accomplishment and personal fulfillment, our work provides an arena for living out our Christian faith. Through conflict, disappointment, and even success, we learn patience and humility. We also learn that people are pretty much the same wherever we go. Everyone has problems, sufferings, and spiritual needs. How we conduct ourselves can either open a door to share the love of Christ, or cause others to say, "If that person's a Christian, I don't want anything to do with it!"

Our work places are, in fact, mission fields where we can daily express actions that reveal the compassions and kindnesses of our Lord. In our interactions with others, we can become the voice and hands of Christ. Even the way we look at a person can convey value and a caring spirit. The old saying is still true: "Actions speak louder than words."

Odd jobs and regular jobs, full and part-time jobs, paid and volunteer jobs—*all* jobs are opportunities to grow spiritually and to spread the fragrance of God's compelling love. Each job teaches us lessons that help make us even more productive in whatever work awaits us during the remaining years of this fleeting life.

Chapter 25

Cool Thoughts ❧

What a difference one degree makes. It can be snowing at our mountain home and raining a thousand feet lower in Leavenworth. The difference? One degree.

Ice will stay ice at 32 degrees. But let the temperature rise a tad and the ice begins to melt.

As a kid, I worked at a marina on Lake Union in Seattle. Big pleasure boats would dock and take on gas and supplies. I'd carry blocks of ice aboard and place them in the ice boxes. On a weekend, I'd lug a ton of ice.

We kept the ice and cans of liquid refreshment in a walk-in "ice house." Inside the door you'd find an ice pick to help break apart the chunks of ice. I would stick the pick in my back pocket in case I needed to chip off some ice to fit the chunk in the on-board fridges.

Then I'd return to the ice house, open the door, and fling the pick toward the ice where, if I was lucky, it would stick in a chunk of ice where I could easily retrieve it for the next load. On occasion I'd miss and penetrate a can of pop or beer, sending fizzy liquid everywhere. The boss failed to see the humor in this.

Sometimes when we have summer guests at our mountain home and our propane refrigerators are full, I'll get a block of ice from a store in town for the ice chest to keep the pop cold.

People put ice cubes in glasses of lemonade and iced tea. Ice packs are used in first aid. We suck on ice chips in the hospital. Driving on ice is treacherous, as is rime ice on the wings of aircraft. Ice is a part of our lives.

Winter ice fishing is a big deal in some places. People drag little sheds onto the ice and sit inside holding a fishing line that drops through a hole in the ice.

In Warsaw, Indiana, enterprising fundraisers would drive a car onto a frozen lake at the height of winter. Then they'd get people to guess the date and time the ice would melt enough for the car to break through. Each guess cost a dollar or two. The winner won a prize and the charity walked away with a pocket full of "donations." I always wondered what happened to the sunken cars.

Ice is a big deal in Leavenworth, Washington. Every winter people come to town to celebrate a festival of ice. An area is designated for artists to carve creations out of ice. The various carvings are judged and winners selected.

Ice carvings are often the centerpieces of fancy buffets. Finely crafted ice houses, ice vehicles, and even ice cities are special attractions in the colder regions of the country. You can do a lot with ice.

We have ice arenas with hockey games and figure skating. I lived in New York City one year and tried to skate at Rockefeller Center during Christmas time. It was a one-time effort, and embarrassing because I couldn't stand up long enough to skate.

Once Sandy was driving on U.S. 30 in Indiana and hit a stretch of black ice. The car spun completely around before coming to a stop.

When we drive to Seattle during the winter we cross over Stevens Pass. More than once I've had trouble keeping our vehicle on the road. Ice can be dangerous.

If I told you I met someone who seemed like a block of ice, you'd know what I meant. You'd picture the person as cold and hard and, well, not very huggable.

How do you change someone like that? How do you melt a cold heart and warm up a frigid relationship?

You can take a sledgehammer and smash the block of ice with pounding condemnation. This only scatters the ice.

You can take a pick and jab at the ice block with criticism. That doesn't work either.

Really, the best way to get rid of ice is to melt it, to change it from a solid to liquid form.

Consider the melting power of a warm and friendly disposition. Kind words and patience radiate a summery glow. Imparting rays of sunlight into one's life can change hardness to softness and coldness to warmth.

Sometimes all it takes is raising the temperature by a single degree—one lifting comment, one thoughtful act, one gesture of good will.

I heard a woman tell of a cold-hearted woman who lived next door. This icy person kept to herself and rejected attempts to befriend her. The neighbor decided to raise the thermostat by small degrees of kindness. She began taking over freshly baked cookies and other pastries. Sometimes she would have to leave them sitting on the porch by the door with a little note.

Sure enough, the chill began to disappear and eventually the two became good friends. All it took was the warmth of human kindness.

Melting cold, hard dispositions brings fresh meaning to our role as lights in the world. Not only are we to disseminate the light of the Gospel, we are also heat lamps, as it were, warming the lives of those around us. Ice melters.

In *The Lion, the Witch and the Wardrobe,* C. S. Lewis tells of a winter land where the wicked witch casts an evil spell on creatures in Narnia, changing them into statues of ice. Along comes Aslan, who breathes on the ice and brings the statues to life. His breath of life liberates them to enjoy the emerging spring.

Is there someone in your life who needs a warm touch, a thawing word, a ray of kindness?

Chapter 26

Breaking Stride ❧

I padded down the country road at a sluggish pace. It was a hot day to be jogging 12 miles. I had never run that far before. But when I passed the 10-mile mark I decided to push on and reach for the big 12.

My feet hurt. My legs weighed 300 pounds. My lungs ached.

As I moved into the final mile I watched an approaching car slow down. The passenger lowered her window.

"Pardon me," she called. "Could you tell us where..."

"I can't stop," I sputtered. And ran on.

Had they been going in my direction, moving along beside me while I ran, I would have helped gladly. But, no, they wanted me to stop, to break stride.

It frustrated me. Couldn't they see I was pouring out my sweat to get somewhere? Didn't they know that you never, ever interrupt a runner?

I made my 12-mile goal standing up. But the accomplishment tasted sour. I kept thinking of the people in the car and my refusal to stop.

It's easy to chase achievement, to be goal-oriented. "Don't bother me; I want to get this done before lunch." "Can't talk now; I'm in a hurry." "Let's make it some other time; I'm too busy this week."

Obsession with reaching our finish lines produces an inflexible pace. Earnestly we pad down the road, panting out words to those who seek our attention: "I can't stop." "I can't talk." "I can't help." "I can't..."

Many goals are worthy. Establishing and maintaining momentum is important. But the good can be twisted. Programs and projects can keep us from people.

Several decades and 45 pounds later, I was jogging again and I had a similar experience with another person seeking information. The car approached and the window went down.

"I'm sorry to bother you," the woman said, "but can you tell me where..."

I stopped. And though the answer to her question was clearly visible on a sign 30 feet away, I took the time to provide directions.

Later, when I finished my run, I felt refreshed and good about myself. I think it had something to do with breaking stride.

The Holy Spirit interrupts us with a word of conviction or a nudge to help someone who is discouraged. Or perhaps it is a question pertaining to our own spiritual life.

We say, "I can't stop now." "I'll do it later." "I'm too busy to pray." We run on keeping pace with the course of this world.

Jesus was heading to Jerusalem to fulfill his mission. Yet, again and again someone interrupted his stride. When blind Bartimaeus cried, "Jesus, Son of David, have mercy on me," the Lord stopped. He was not too busy, too wrapped up in his own goals, to pause and help this man.

When I was a kid working my way through the preteen years, a student at Seattle Pacific College took time to befriend me. I was nothing to him, but for some reason he broke his stride for me.

I think of another student who invited me to go home with him to meet his younger brother who was my age...and the friendship that developed out of that.

Then there's the list of Sunday school teachers and Boy Scout leaders who stopped to offer friendship and guidance. When I think of it, my life is full of those who cared enough about a young man to break stride and offer help.

I read a booklet one time titled, "The Tyranny of the Urgent." It drew a distinction between truly important things and those lesser things we allow to control our time and energies. The writer challenged the readers to keep their priorities straight and to focus attention on the kingdom of God and on doing what really counts.

I'm also thinking of a report I once read in *Psychology Today*. Students were told that the Dean wanted to see them. On the way to the Dean's office, the unknowing student would come across a distressed student who had been planted in a strategic location. I forget the problem, but it was obvious enough to attract attention and require assistance.

Some students were individually told that the Dean was expecting them in five minutes. Others were told they had 30 minutes. Overwhelmingly, the students with more time to reach their destination stopped to assist the "hurting" student. The others hurried by to make their appointment.

The Parable of the Good Samaritan is also instructive. We don't know about any time constraints, but we do know those who should have stopped rushed by without getting involved.

As you "run the race" today and come upon someone who could use a kind deed or encouraging word, will you run past? What about that older person who is struggling with health issues or a dwindling income? Will you break stride?

Are you willing to stop and get on eye-level with a youngster and say something to enlighten or affirm?

Personal goals and time constraints will try to push us past young, old, and many in between who appear before us on the roadway of life.

Jesus stopped. What about you and me?

Losing Cause

I am a reluctant friend of diet plans. Over the years I've done Weight Watchers®, Slim Fast®, South Beach®, Jenny Craig®, NutriSystem®—to name a few. Once, when I was editorial director of a publishing house in the Midwest, I corralled a small group of fellow workers and challenged them to join me in a weight-loss program. We promised to meet daily (M-F) in my office for a brown bag lunch.

At the noon hour, a half dozen calorie-counters filed into my office and sat down in a half-circle of chairs. Out of the bags we drew hard-boiled eggs, cheese sticks, celery, and other kinds of rabbit food. As we munched, we each reported our eating activities over the previous 24 hours. We held each other accountable for walking the line and poured on encouragement where needed.

Sometimes our conversations became quite serious as we probed each other regarding our weight problems and past efforts to conquer the battle of the bulge. I recall one large woman who struggled with her self-image as she began to lose weight. She was afraid of what she was becoming. She said, "I know me as I am now but not what I will look like when I lose weight." She dropped out of the program after a couple of weeks.

Over the course of time, we did pretty well and our success was noted by other employees. Our lunch meetings became celebratory. We laughed together and awarded each other with enthusiastic high-fives as we inched toward our individual goals.

When someone felt he or she needed to quit the group for one reason or another, it kind of deflated the rest of us. Finally, with only three of us remaining, we decided to officially disband and keep working on our goals by ourselves.

You can imagine what happened. Within a few months we were back on the eating trail and the good work of our weight-loss efforts evaporated. Old patterns of undisciplined eating regained control.

Several years later, I joined a Prism® weight-loss group at our church. At the first session, we launched a new and guaranteed-to-work program to overcome our lust for chocolate. We all did amazingly well and I found myself at the head of the class. My unwanted pounds dropped off like leaves in an autumn wind.

After losing 40 pounds, I thought of a brilliant idea to demonstrate my success in a way that might encourage the others. I went to the beach near our house and collected a few bags of sand. Then I took a backpack and placed it on a scale and filled it with 40-pounds of sand.

At the next meeting, I set the pack on the floor in the middle of the circle of chairs. During the reporting phase of the meeting, I asked one of the ladies to go over and lift up the pack. She couldn't lift it. Another person tried and barely got it off the floor. Then I exclaimed, "That's how much weight I've lost on this diet!"

I encouraged them to stay with the program and lose their own backpack of pounds. The object lesson hit home and for the next few weeks the class excelled in determination and enthusiasm.

But, again, the long-term outcome made it difficult for members of the class to look each other in the eye. I think it's fair to say that by the same time a year later most of us were eating candy again.

In my experiences as a diet aficionado, I began to realize that part of the problem many of us face is a lack of will power in the afternoon and evening. As the day wears on, our discipline wanes and we are inextricably drawn to the cupboard for snacks, or to the freezer where the ice cream waits.

As I mulled this over, a grand idea burst on my mind: If I could provide dieters with immediate access to words of encouragement, perhaps this would help them get through those tough times of temptation when visions of cookies danced in their minds. What if a teetering dieter could pick up the phone and call a number to get a pep talk that would see them through the crisis?

It that moment, "Losing Cause" was born.

The name said it all: A failsafe cause to help dieting failures make it into the end zone of skinniness. Little did I realize at the time that the name would have another meaning as well.

Once I got Sandy tuned into the idea, I ordered a separate phone line and purchased a top-of-the-line phone message machine. Then I recorded a one-minute message not unlike the rantings of a football coach at half-time. I prepared 20 of these segments, including homemade poetry, singing, and slapstick humor. A five-second tag line gave a box number and requested financial support. I advertised in the local newspaper.

Each day I changed the message. Twenty days later, I started over. My plan was to go through three cycles and then decided whether or not to continue.

When the newspaper ad came out, the phone started to ring. The pace quickened over the next several days and soon the machine was logging more than a hundred calls. I heard reports from friends who heard from others. It was quite exciting to hear the phone ring in the middle of the night and imagine that some poor distraught dieter would be lifted out of defeat.

I also learned that "Losing Cause" became something of a joke. For example, someone would scribble a note and place it on a co-worker's desk, "Please call _____." The unsuspecting worker would dial and be blasted with a robust pep talk or a song for shedding pounds.

Alas, my surefire plan became a losing cause. After two months, we cancelled the phone line and put the program behind us. Sandy was kind enough not to rub it in.

I only received one piece of mail in the PO Box during those two months. The envelope contained two pennies and this note: "This is for the two pounds I lost."

Those who deal with the ongoing challenge of maintaining healthy eating habits will empathize with my experiences. They know all about the cycle of losing-gaining-losing. They know what it requires to take it off and keep it off.

For most of us, maintaining a healthy spiritual life can also be a challenge. We have learned that there are no shortcuts, no easy programs to keep us fit and effective for the Lord. That is why we keep coming back to the tried and true "means of grace." We depend on:

1. Daily prayer, meaning conscious communion with God in private and communal settings.
2. Daily Bible reading, including personal study, memorization, and meditation.
3. Regular worship with other believers and participation in the Lord's Supper.
4. Fellowship with other believers, including small group meetings.
5. Ongoing service and witness to others, both within and without the church family.

Christians who settle for moral junk food and consume the "sweets" of a godless culture accumulate needless weight and suffer spiritual sluggishness. Disregarding God's call to discipleship, they gain the poundage of guilt and regret.

God calls us to leanness in worldly attachments and agility in matters of the heart. We are to feed on the "manna" he provides and daily exercise our spiritual muscles. We are to drink often from the well of salvation and follow closely the directives of our heavenly Trainer. He gives us the will to keep going and the energy to prevail. We are his disciples, men and women who live healthy and productive lives for the glory of his name.

While we may lack victory in the physical arena of life, we can experience the ongoing joy of spiritual health as we walk in the strength of the Lord. And as we do, we find the resilience, strength, and determination to keep battling whatever human maladies we endure, including the ongoing struggle to gain and maintain lean and healthy bodies.

Chapter 28

When Mom Stomped Out

Sometimes grownups act weird. Take my mother and me, for example. The two of us once drove a convertible from Detroit to Seattle without stopping—every mile with the top down. Another time we put on a skit at a fancy banquet. Here's the story:

For several years, my family and my parents lived in Winona Lake, Indiana. At that time, the little town was the location for the World Headquarters of the Free Methodist Church of North America. My dad was the executive secretary for Higher Education and the Ministry and I was editor of the denomination's official publication, *Light and Life Magazine.*

Every year the headquarters executives and spouses held a Christmas banquet to award service pins and to honor retiring personnel. The program committee asked if I might provide a skit or monologue to spice up the evening. I said, "Let me think about it."

Years before, I had played the trombone and often my mother would accompany me on the piano. The idea of a skit with the trombone might draw some laughs, so I checked with my mom and gave the committee the green light.

I had lived in the community for several years and had not played the trombone once. So when word leaked out that I was going to play a solo at the banquet, several people said something like, "I'm glad to hear you're getting back into the trombone."

The big night came and the place was packed. All five bishops were there with their spouses. The meal was delightful and table conversations filled the air. Finally, with dessert out of the way, the MC made a few valiant efforts at humor. Then he announced that I would play a medley of songs on my trombone. A few muffled expressions of surprise reached my ears. My hands became clammy.

My mother rose and went to the grand piano. I retrieved the trombone and took my place near the piano where I faced a sea of anticipatory faces.

Mom, who was an accomplished pianist, played a stirring introduction, complete with a rolling arpeggio. A slight pause indicated my turn to play. As I raised the instrument to my lips, I discovered that the mouthpiece was not there. It was in my pocket where it would keep warm. I had failed to affix it to the trombone and so I stood there feigning embarrassment. Issuing appropriate apologies, I put the mouthpiece in place and motioned to my mother to play the introduction again.

Again, the arpeggio and the moment of my first sound. I moved the slide into position. Unfortunately, I went too far out with the slide and it came off the two tubes. I stood there with the trombone in one hand and the slide in the other. My apologies rose to new heights and I said something about being nervous since I hadn't performed in a long time.

A few snickers rose from the crowd, but most people seemed to empathize with me and share my embarrassment.

Once again I nodded to my mother and again she filled the room with a marvelous introduction. This time, when I blew into the mouthpiece, nothing came out. Something was plugging the flow of air.

Apologizing profusely, I took off the upper tuning slide and found that a rag had been stuffed in the tube. I said, "I think I know who did this and when I get home I'm going to have something to say to my children. This is not funny and I am so sorry to be messing up your evening."

By now most of the crowd was catching on. Still, I spotted a few puzzled faces.

"Mom," I said, "let's try it again. I don't know what else could go wrong."

Once more she played the introduction and with great flourish rolled off the arpeggio. I lifted the horn to my mouth and tried to move the slide into position. It wouldn't budge. "It's locked," I said, "I forgot to unlock it. Play it again, Mom."

With that she stood up, grabbed her music, and stomped out of the room in a huff. I followed her out, pleading with her to return and try again.

When we re-entered the room, the crowd greeted us with laughter and applause. It seemed like everyone was having a great time.

Well, not everyone. I learned that one of the bishop's wives said to others at the table, "I fail to see the humor in this." And she was dead serious. She went on to chastise those around her for making fun of me. She sincerely thought my troubles were unintentional. Her husband and a few others at the table were able to bring her around...and then she was embarrassed at her failure to "get the joke."

A few years later my mother passed away. She left me with so many fun memories that it's hard not to chuckle when I think of them—especially the night she accompanied me at the headquarters Christmas banquet.

When I think about that skit, I'm reminded of times in my life when things didn't go just right. One thing after another happened to turn the situation into a comedy of errors. Like the bishop's wife (long ago deceased) I tend to take things too seriously and fail to enjoy the peculiarities and happenstances of life.

Sometimes we just need to lean back and laugh at ourselves. We also need to reaffirm our confidence in the sovereignty of God and his amazing ability to make all things "work together for good."

Chapter 29

Goodbye, Old Friend

My first trombone was a school instrument, a beat-up thing I learned to play well enough to be in our grade school orchestra. When my folks saw me enjoying the slush pump, they bought me a new one and urged me to excel.

It was really neat—all shiny and nestled in a brand new case. And did that slide work! I had to maintain a good grip so as not to lose the slider when I went out there to 7th position.

I played through junior high and high school, blaring away at football games, marching and playing at parades, holding forth in orchestra, swing band, even the all-city youth orchestra.

I recall marching in the Seafair Parade one year, down through the middle of Seattle. First row, on the end. About half way through I got an excruciating side ache. While the band played on, I hunch over and stumbled along in pain. It was embarrassing, to say the least. Fortunately the ache subsided and I was again able to put the mouthpiece to my lips.

For a time I took lessons from a band teacher and seasoned trombonist. Later I tried to learn from the first chair trombonist of the Seattle Symphony. Along the way I started playing solos. I performed all through college and graduate school.

Once I played for a room full of young teens. It was a camp setting and I was the special music before the speaker. As I played, I noticed that the audience began to giggle and poke each other. They became more animated as I continued. I could actually hear snickers and outright guffaws.

I was hitting my notes and doing an OK job...so why were they laughing? While trying to remember the next note, I went through a checklist of things that might be causing amusement: Unzipped fly? Funny posture? Awkward slide action? The possible causes piled up in my mind, and yet I pushed on, eager to reach the last note.

As they continued to poke each other and laugh, I wanted to hurl my trombone at them and bolt for the door. But in my humiliation, I played on. It was the worst experience of my solo-playing life.

Finally I finished and took my seat. It was then I saw the squirrel on the top of the curtain rod at the back of the stage. While I was playing, the little rascal had climbed up the curtain and walked back and forth across the top.

I thought they were all laughing at me, when in reality they were laughing at the antics of the furry creature behind me. I took it personally, but the focus was not me at all. I jumped to a false conclusion because I didn't have all the facts. Their laughter had nothing to do with me!

I loved my trombone so much I took it with me up to a Forest Service fire lookout where I spent the summer of '57. I'd stand out on the catwalk and serenade the marmots with "Sweet

Georgia Brown." I even played a tune over the two-way radio once, to the disgust of the district ranger.

You know how runners talk about reaching that point where ecstasy sets in and they feel like they can run forever? That's the way I felt about practicing. I'd hole up in a practice room and play for hours, losing myself in the exhilaration of improvising whatever came to mind. I'm sure I played through the hymnbook more than once.

But, alas, the time came when practicing diminished and the lips went limp. Family life and work responsibilities assumed prominence and I let the trombone slide (so to speak). Finally, after several years of increasing neglect, I stored my horn in the garage.

A brief awakening came when my son entered middle school and wanted to play an instrument. I retrieved the old bone and, between stories of the glory days, helped him get started. He stuck with it for a few years, and then his interests turned elsewhere. The horn went back to the garage.

Whenever we had a garage sale, my wife would inquire about the trombone. "Shall we sell it? Has the time come?" And always I would say, "No, let's hang on to it. Maybe someday I'll start playing again."

One fateful afternoon a dozen years ago, Sandy and I cleaned out the garage and put a few things on the driveway with a "For Sale" sign in front. We came across the trombone and she asked "What about this?"

I gulped and said, "The trombone?"

She said, "Is it time to say goodbye?"

I said, "Okay, let's do it."

I set the case on a little table near the road and opened it to display the contents. A lump formed in my throat. I sighed and thought, *I sure don't want to get rid of this horn. But the time has come.* I taped a little sign to the case: "$25.00."

Two boys were walking their bikes up the street and came over to take a look. "Wow," said one. "That's a good deal. Does it work?" I told them about it and when I began to reminisce, they left.

At the end of the day the unsold horn went back to the garage. Saved again.

The next afternoon, the mother of one of the boys called to inquire about the trombone. Apparently, the lad had gone home and pleaded for his folks to buy him the instrument. He was, I thought, the same age I had been when I started playing.

Soon the boy was standing with me in the garage while his father waited in the car. I opened the case and assembled the trombone. Puckering up, I blatted out a few notes and moved the slide up and down. "See, it still works." I showed him the mute and music holder and several sheets of music that were in the case.

I told him this could be the beginning of great things for him if he practiced and practiced. I said, "Keep the money; I want to give you the trombone. And maybe someday if you ever give a recital or play in a concert, you'll come back and let me know."

I watched in the darkness of the garage as he carried the case to the car and placed it in the back seat. I felt sadness in my heart. I may have offered a little prayer for the boy and his horn.

It was only a dented and scratched metal contraption in a broken-down case. Yes, but an instrument I had breathed life into again and again, one I had poured my heart through to make music for myself and others.

Silly though it seems, the gift of that horn nearly moved me to tears. It represented special times in my life and many associations.

Now, years later, I still think about that trombone. And, yes, I do get the urge to find a used horn and play for my own amusement. But I tell myself those days are gone and there are other ways to make music.

I think, for example, of the ministry of writing the Lord has given me. Words instead of notes pour out of my life and reach a far larger audience than my trombone ever did. I also think of "solos" I can play in helping those who need a word of encouragement or a helping hand. Or performing duets of service with my wife or another believer?

Life moves on and there are always new opportunities and ministries waiting for us to become an instrument in the Lord's hands.

One thing I learned about playing the trombone is the importance of practice. I had to spend hours in private before I could minister effectively in public. How true this is of our calling to be effective witnesses and servants of Christ. We must spend time in the closet, learning the notes of Scripture and developing clear and heart-filled tones through prayer and meditation.

We are all part of God's marching band and that means practice and preparation for the stirring music the world is waiting to hear. It means following the Drum Major and performing our part with precision and an upbeat spirit—even when we don't feel like it.

And what a band it is! Far more than 76 Trombones!

Chapter 30

Two Batons ❧

North Queen Anne Grade School sat next to an athletic field that included a quarter-mile track. On special occasions, we would have all-school activities on the field and participate in various track events. I had long legs as a seventh grader and could generate considerable speed. And I loved to run.

One of my favorite races was the relay event. Teams of four would space themselves evenly around the track and a starting gun would send the first group sprinting toward their replacements. Because of my speed, I was usually the fourth runner, the team anchor.

As the third runner rounded the track and sprinted toward me, I'd begin running so when he reached me we were both nearly side-by-side. In that moment, he would reach out the baton and I would grab it and shift into overdrive for the last portion of the race.

Timing and accuracy in grasping the baton demanded concentration and skill, and woe to runners who failed to make the exchange successfully.

Sometimes the third runner would fail to reach out the baton correctly or would slow down prematurely. Perhaps the anchor failed to grasp the rod tightly and dropped it in the process. Or maybe both runners botched the exchange. Whatever the case, once the baton hit the cinders, you could kiss victory goodbye.

Thoughts of those early years on the grade-school track came back to me during the weeks following my father's death in 2010. During the day and night preceding his last breath I sat next to his bed, holding his hand and comforting him with words of Scripture and well-loved hymns. Although he didn't open his eyes or speak to me, I felt an occasional squeeze that let me know he was aware of my presence.

In those squeezes, it was as though he were handing me a baton. "Here, son, I'm running out of strength. My life is nearly gone. Take the baton and run your part of the race well. Go flat out for the finish line and keep your eyes on the goal. Don't be distracted or fall by the wayside. Keep the faith. Run with patience."

As part of his estate, I received another baton from my dad—the one he used to direct choral groups. With this baton, he started and stopped the choir, kept time, provided cues, and generally directed the singers. Facial expressions, posture, and motions of the left hand augmented the movement of the baton.

Although he was an effective college administrator and president, his first love was music and he always found a way to be involved with choirs.

On one of our visits to see him at a retirement community, I found him directing a choir of senior residents in "God so Loved the World." They were practicing for their first public presentation at church on Palm Sunday. I was amazed how, at 93, he could bring such splendid music out of this older group—many of whom had sung in his choirs in bygone years.

After they were done, I said, "Dad, you still have the golden touch."

I actually took a course in choral conducting from my father at college. In the process I learned that leading a choir or instrumental group involved a whole lot more than just standing up there waving your arms.

The final exam required each of us to stand before the others (the "choir") and conduct a choral selection. My dad marked us for posture, motion, interpretation, and other elements. We had to have the musical score memorized so we could focus on the singers and cue the different voice sections at appropriate times. My selection was "All in the April Evening." I used his baton.

Although I did go on to direct choirs now and then, I was never a maestro like my dad. I could never do what he did in music or, for that matter, in college administration. He had his course of service and I have mine.

Each one of us has two batons. We carry the baton of personal faith and obedience, running with perseverance the race set before us. And we carry the baton of service and leadership, drawing praise to God out of those we engage along the way.

Two batons: One for running the race; the other for offering service. One for God; one for others. Faith and works.

So it is with every generation of God's children. We receive the baton from godly forerunners of the Faith and we take our turn, running our course for the glory of God. And as we run, we minister to the needs of others.

I've been thinking of those qualities and virtues in my father's life that he placed in my care requiring my stewardship and emulation. Things like moral integrity, loyalty, diligence, devotion, fiscal responsibility, good humor, and concern for others. These comprise a heavy baton and I trust in God that I am able to carry it well and to "run and not grow weary."

I trust also that, figuratively, I will be able to wield his baton of music in a way that I can draw out of others the oratorios of faith, the anthems of praise, and the hymns of love for our Lord and Savior, Jesus Christ. I want my family and friends to dwell in harmony and to live melodious lives.

In both our running and leading, let us honor those who have gone before and who now join with other saints in the grandstands above us, urging us on to the very day when we hand off our batons—faith in Christ and service to others.

About the Author

During my life I have had a variety of jobs and involvements. I've served as lead pastor, college prof, Bible teacher, foundation director, editorial director, business owner, freelance writer, editor, and consultant in philanthropic planning.

I've enjoyed many outdoor experiences, including hiking, snowmobiling, off-roading, fishing, piloting land and sea planes, river-running, and international travel.

I'm now "retired" and live with my lovely wife in Wenatchee, on the eastern side of the Cascade Mountains. Our four incredible children are married to wonderful spouses and we have terrific grandchildren. (Pardon the superlatives.)

For 15 years we lived "off the grid" eight miles from the Bavarian village of Leavenworth, Washington. Tucked into Icicle Canyon, we were encircled by the Alpine Lakes Wilderness Area. It was unspeakably beautiful there and I sometimes wondered whether we had somehow stumbled into the Garden of Eden.

As I have shared some of my experiences through word and print, friends have encouraged me to put them in book form. The present volume resulted from that impetus. Other books—print and/or electronic—have been published or are in process. You can learn about these by visiting my website at www.papathree.com.

As you read the stories in this book, I trust you will be nourished in your heart and inspired to live all-out for God. There are many adventures in life, but the greatest of all is in knowing and serving the Lord Jesus Christ.

—*G. Roger Schoenhals*

Devotional Publications By the Author

Chained to Paul
    —Exploring Philippians Link By Link
Awake My Soul
    —Devotional Readings in Colossians
Jonah, A Devotional Journey
Deeper in the Lord's Prayer
    —Thirty Days of Discovery
In the Psalms, A New Beginning
    —Daily Meditations for Two Weeks
In the Psalms Along the Way
    —Daily Meditations for Three Months
In the Psalms Beside Still Waters
    —Daily Meditations for Three Months
In the Psalms Day by Day
    —Daily Meditations for Three Months
In the Psalms in Hard Places
    —Daily Meditations for Three Months
Hikes, Flights, and Lookout Stories
    —Life Lessons From High Places
Dogs, Camping, and Other Candid Tales
    —Life Lessons From the Out-of-Doors
Saga of the Red Truck
    —Life Lessons From Here and There

For the most current information, visit
the author's website at www.papathree.com.

Contact Information

To order additional copies of this book, please visit
www.redemption-press.com.
Also available on Amazon.com and BarnesandNoble.com
Or by calling toll free 1-844-2REDEEM.

CPSIA information can be obtained
at www.ICGtesting.com
Printed in the USA
FSOW01n1135230316
18198FS